"Like the rest of his stuff, Matthew Paul Turner's latest is a fun combo of solid advice, good humor, and entertaining commentary. Reading it is like hanging out with your funny, cool, been-there-done-that older brother."

— JASON BOYETT, author of *Pocket Guide to Adulthood* and *Pocket Guide to the Bible*

"I am recommending this book to every high school graduate I know! It's a fantastic resource."

— DANIEL EAGAN, student ministries director, Riverside Presbyterian Church

"This guide to college life is certain to make a difference for any reader and save a lot of grief at the same time. Not just a guide to surviving, it is a blueprint for thriving in the new world beyond high school. This fun and energetic read will keep you engaged and turning the pages!"

— BETHEL THOMAS JR., PhD, vice president for university advancement, Belmont University

A STUDENT'S SURVIVAL GUIDE

EVERYTHING
YOU NEED TO KNOW BEFORE
COLLEGE

MATTHEW PAUL TURNER

THiNK
P.O. Box 35001
Colorado Springs, Colorado 80935

THiNK is an imprint of NavPress.

THiNK and the THiNK logo are registered trademarks of NavPress. Absence of ® in connection with marks of NavPress or other parties does not indicate an absence of registration of those marks.

ISBN 1-57683-973-7

Cover and interior design by studiogearbox.com
Cover photo by CSA Plastock
Creative Team: Nicci Hubert, Judith Wilson, Kathy Mosier, Arvid Wallen, Pat Reinheimer

Turner, Matthew Paul, 1973-
  Everything you need to know before college / Matthew Paul Turner.
    p. cm.
  Includes bibliographical references (p.   ).
  ISBN 1-57683-973-7
  1. High school graduates--Religious life. 2. Christian college
students--Religious life. I. Title.
  BV4531.3.T87 2006
  248.8'34--dc22
                          2006007807

Printed in the United States of America

1 2 3 4 5 6 7 8 9 10 / 10 09 08 07 06

FOR A FREE CATALOG OF NAVPRESS BOOKS & BIBLE STUDIES,
CALL 1-800-366-7788 (USA) OR 1-800-839-4769 (CANADA)

CONTENTS

ACKNOWLEDGMENTS

I WOULD LIKE TO THANK:

My parents: for good genes. I mean, seriously; good genes are really hard to come by these days.

My sisters: for not taking all the good genes. All three of you are such good sharers.

My brothers-in-law: for noticing my sisters' good genes.

My nieces and nephews: for carrying the good genes on and for making me smile.

My friends: for making life interesting, for being humble and funny, and for sending me all your great college stories.

My college professors: yeah, like any of you are going to read this book.

My alma mater, Belmont: for accepting me despite my pathetic SAT scores.

My editor, Nicci: for inviting me to take part; this was fun.

My publisher, NavPress: for welcoming me on board, but more important, for truly caring about college students.

My interviewees: for sharing your wisdom with us.

My iPod: for allowing me to take all of my favorite songs with me wherever I go.

My wife: for the good lovin' and for thinking my genes were hot enough to marry.

INTRODUCTION

(Because every book needs one, or at least that's what I've been told)

WOW. YOU FINISHED HIGH school. Your soul should be welled up with pride, don't you think? Don't get too carried away, though. I'm not asking you to make a complete idol of yourself. Nobody wants you acting like you are walking the red carpet at the MTV Video Music Awards. You're not exactly Gwen Stefani.

But you should definitely be excited about what you've accomplished. Graduating from high school is a big deal. So take a moment and revel in the feeling. Throw a party, hang out with a bunch of your friends and family, let your relatives give you large sums of cash and gift cards to Wal-Mart, eat some cake, and drink a Sprite or two. (If you're into a bit more dazzle, add a little cherry juice for effect.)

Oh, and let your momma take lots of pictures of you with your dad, grandparents, and friends. You'll thank her ten years from now for making you stand there smiling like a complete idiot wearing that awful cap and gown. Or, if the pictures turn out horrible, you might end up hating her. But I think you'll eventually get over that.

So I might have lost a few of you with those first few paragraphs. There's a decent chance that not *all* of you reading this book have finished high school yet. *Poor things. Believe us; we all understand your pain.*

For those of you who are still wading your way through the homework, bad school lunches, peer pressure, pep rallies, and gym class—hang in there. The end of high school will come soon enough.

I promise that all of the hard work will be worth it. Just ask all of those *former students* you know who have already walked the aisle of their school gymnasium or auditorium to the music of the slowest song in the world, "Pomp and Circumstance." I bet they'll tell you it felt pretty darn good. In fact, even students who are seemingly irritated all of the time might actually crack a smile when they talk about finishing high school. I can't remember *ever* meeting a student who didn't have one of those big stupid grins smacked on his or her face come graduation night.

Whether you've finished high school or not, if you've picked up this book then you're no doubt planning to attend college, or you're *thinking* about attending college, *or* someone you love is trying desperately to get you to seriously think about attending college. And unlike the other books about college that are three inches thick and read like Moses-written encyclopedias (I mean, he did write Leviticus), you might actually *read* this one, or at least parts of it.

At least, that's my hope.

Okay, back to college. As you've probably heard your entire life, college is a must if you want to be successful in life, accomplish all of your dreams, make something of yourself, and all those other clichés we tell ourselves so we'll be excited about going to college. But seriously, all of those clichés are pretty much true. Sure, there are a few exceptions to the rule—people who have no formal college education yet eventually become influential leaders or successful business-women or wealthy inventors. But for most of us—the you and me crowd—college is a must. So that's why we attend.

Of course, people attend college for different reasons. Some simply go in hopes of getting through the four years of school as fast as possible so they can *make it* in the business world or education world. Some go to college just to figure out what they want to do with the rest of their lives. Others go for a change of scenery, hoping their *escape* will save them from the ordinary lives their hometowns offer. Many attend college to learn specific trades, skills, or professions. From sports to partying to finding a spouse to spiritual growth to gaining knowledge, the reasons people go to college are endless, really.

But almost all people who attend college have one thing in common: They go hoping that their experience will make them smarter and more emotionally mature and will lead them to success.

Doesn't that last sentence sound absolutely dreamy? Perfect? *Nauseating?* Forgive me; I sometimes write content that would probably be better suited for the last three minutes of a *Full House* episode. Imagine how Danny Tanner (played by Bob Saget) would have approached those words: "Oh, DJ, your college education is supposed to grow you mentally and emotionally so that you will be better prepared for success in life. Nobody said it would be perfect, but . . ." Can you hear the cheesy theme music?

Okay, back to non-sitcom thinking.

I truly believe that college is one of the most memorable and important times in a person's existence. It will grow you in ways you cannot imagine. Without a doubt, it should be an experience worth remembering, holding on to, and taking with you into whatever life may hold. (Yeah, I know; that was another *Full House* moment.)

The book you're holding, *Everything You Need to Know Before College*, will help you make the most of your experience. It's not simply a book about procedures and guides. In this book, I have written information meant to help you pursue a *whole* college experience. And *whole* includes not only what you'll learn in the classroom; it encompasses all that you will encounter—from relationships to ministries to professors to parties. It's all a part of the college adventure.

Your guide for the next 200ish pages,

MATTHEW PAUL TURNER

matthew@dottedline.net
www.MatthewPaulTurner.com

A LITTLE STORY
BEFORE YOU BEGIN . . .

THREE MONTHS SHY OF turning eighteen, I walked into my first college classroom. My first impression was positive; in fact, it was nearly shockingly positive. The lighting in the room was soft, almost warm and inviting. There were no fluorescent lights shining down from the ceiling like I had experienced in high school. No obnoxious, studious-appearing décor on the walls, either. The classroom was clean and inviting. With its large plush chairs and long uniform tables that ran the length of the room, the scene seemed to be what I would have imagined a large corporate meeting room to be like.

With a heavy book bag hanging on one shoulder and my blue and white high school letterman jacket warming me against the outside's cool fall air, I anxiously and curiously entered my first college experience. Looking around the large room, much larger than I had been accustomed to in high school, I began to contemplate where I should sit. I had been told by a couple of my older and supposedly "wiser" friends that this was an important decision.

My friends told me that where I chose to sit would play a significant role in what type of student my professors would perceive me to be. Knowing that I was an average learner with some noticeable symptoms of ADHD, I decided to sit at about midway back, a little left of center. That way, I wasn't a kiss-up or a slacker.

I quietly approached my seat.

As I began to sit down, my quiet moment ended when my thirty-five-pound book bag heavily flopped off my left shoulder, smacking violently against the tiled floor. The sound announced to the room that I had arrived. The girl sitting directly behind me yelped as if she had actually *been* the floor.

"OH MY GOSH!" she exclaimed. Her voice echoing through the room was nearly as loud as the sound my book bag had made. "What are you trying to do, put a gaping hole in the center of the room?" she bellowed.

I didn't respond.

"DID YOU HEAR ME?" she asked, while simultaneously leaning over the table in front of her and tapping her pointer finger against my back.

She's touching me, I thought. *Yuck.*

As I turned around, I thought I had this girl's type pegged. My mental picture resembled a *Cosmo*-influenced diva trying to manipulate her territory. But I was *way* off. When I turned around to look at her, I realized I was giving her way too much credit. She was more like a pudgy Cindy Lauper with an obvious knack for exaggerating a predicament.

When our eyes met, she spoke.

"Don't you think you're making an awful lot of noise for the first day of school?" she asked quite frankly.

Neither a smile nor a frown covered her face, which didn't help me understand whether she was being serious or toying with someone she had never met.

"Are you talking to me?" I asked with a grin.

"OF COURSE, I'M TALKING TO YOU," she snapped, her nasally tone scraped against my eardrums. "YOU are the one making all the noise, RIGHT?"

"I'm sorry I disturbed you," I said with as much sincerity as I could muster up.

The troublemaker, who was my first college acquaintance, just stared at me quizzically. Her eyes moved fast, up and down from my face to my chest to the book bag that was now *quietly* sitting on the floor next to my chair. I turned back around in my desk, but I could still feel the weight of her glare.

Suddenly, the girl tapped her finger against my back—*again*.

"Yes?"

"I know I don't know you, but I have to ask: Has anyone ever told you that you look exactly like Matthew Broderick?"

Sadly, because of my strict religious past, which said it was sinful for me to go to movies, I had never heard the name Matthew Broderick.

"No, I have never been told that," I said. "Who is he?" My lack of pop-cultural knowledge caused her to shriek yet again.

"YOU DON'T KNOW MATTHEW BRODERICK?" the girl asked with complete shock.

"No, I'm afraid not," I said, feeling rather uncool and a little bit sweaty.

"YOU'VE NEVER SEEN THE MOVIE *FERRIS BUELLER'S DAY OFF*?"

"I guess not."

"HE'S THE STAR OF THAT MOVIE. . . .YOU HAVE GOT TO SEE THAT MOVIE," she screeched. "YOU *LOOK* JUST LIKE HIM!"

By this time, because my new friend had a tendency to be loud, many in the room were being entertained by the exchange of dialogue. In fact, a few joined the conversation with an array of comments.

"You do kind of look like him," said one girl.

"You even wear a letterman jacket like him," said another.

"I thought the movie was stupid; you didn't miss anything," said one of the smart guys in the front row.

It seemed that almost everyone of the sixty or so students in the room had an opinion or comment. Without trying and without my permission, my resemblance to an actor I did not know caused me to become the center of the room's attention. And unbeknownst to me at the time, during those first few minutes, while the class awaited the professor's arrival into the classroom, my entire first year of college would be somewhat affected by one girl's thoughts, words, and weird influence.

"I HAVE AN IDEA!" she yelled. "I PROPOSE THAT FROM NOW ON WE CALL YOU FERRIS!"

"What?" I laughed. "My name's Matthew. I think we should just stick to that."

"OH MY GOSH! YOUR NAME IS MATTHEW? JUST LIKE THE REAL FERRIS BUELLER! THAT MAKES IT EVEN MORE PERFECT. THAT SETTLES IT: YOU ARE OFFICIALLY FERRIS!!!!!"

Several people began to laugh in agreement. They looked at me and nodded their heads as if to say, "Yep, your name is now Ferris."

Unfortunately, I didn't have a say in the matter. So I just smiled and assumed that my new moniker would probably not last past this first class. But my new friend was persistent. By the third class, most of my fellow students didn't even know my *real* name; they simply knew me as Ferris. But it wasn't simply students in that class who officially called me Ferris. Other classes caught wind of the nickname and began to use it. Even that first class's professor, after a bit of coaxing from the students, eventually began referring to me as Ferris. Strangers would run up to me on campus and say, "You're the guy they call Ferris, right?" For that entire first year, long after that class was completed, I was known to most at Chesapeake College as simply Ferris.

And to be honest, despite it being a little annoying at first, a part of me kind of liked it.

SOME PRACTICAL ADVICE
(To make college life a little easier on the back)

Don't buy a cheap book bag. Usually, anything less than thirty-five dollars is not going to last and will do more harm than good. With the weight of life on your back (literally), you need to invest in a book bag that will help that heavy load not cause havoc on your spine, shoulders, and neck. When thinking book bags, choose carefully, much like you would choose a comfortable pair of shoes. Brands to consider: Jansport, North Face, L.L.Bean, and Columbia. Be prepared to spend between forty and seventy dollars. When you're thirty-five, you will thank me.

I learned a lot on that first day at Chesapeake College, a small community college on the Eastern Shore of Maryland. Much deeper than just learning that I looked a lot like some famous guy I should have known, I also learned a few more important things about college life. Sure, my college was small, and yes, I did drive home to Mom and Dad's later that afternoon. But nonetheless, that first day certainly opened my eyes to the struggles, joys, hard work, life changes, and so much more that would soon enough become *my life* during the next five years. Here's a quick look at what I learned on my first day of college.

FIVE THINGS I LEARNED* ON THE FIRST DAY OF COLLEGE

1. COLLEGE PROFESSORS ARE DIFFERENT FROM HIGH SCHOOL TEACHERS

In high school, most teachers really get into helping you become a good student—that's a part of their job. But in college, the professors are being paid to know a particular subject, topic, procedure, or event. Unfortunately, people skills are *optional*. The help they offer after class or on weekends is considered voluntary. Although some of my professors were quite helpful when I struggled my way through a class, it was not in their job description to encourage me not to procrastinate or to read *all* my material, and they didn't call my parents when I wasn't performing well.

On that first day, one of my professors looked at the class and touted, "I'm not here to babysit you; I'm here to teach a class. So please don't waste my time with silly questions. If you need help with my class, my study guide is available in the library. So go find it there." That professor proved he was about as likable as Joseph Stalin. I learned quickly not to depend on a professor to make college easier or convenient for me.

---

* Although I believe you will experience similar first-day lessons, like most of life, results vary greatly by location, personality, school, and frankly, your overall ability to function.

2. THE MEANING OF THE WORD SYLLABUS

Sadly, when the professor began talking about the syllabus, I had no clue what the word meant. At the time, I thought it might be some kind of rare STD that I had never heard about. So I turned to the person on my left and asked, "What's a syllabus?" I felt better when my neighbor looked at me and shrugged her shoulders. However, by the end of the first day, I had a new word in my vocabulary.

Just in case you're like me and don't know the meaning of the word *syllabus*, here's how Dictionary.com defines the word: "An outline or a summary of the main points of a text, lecture, or course of study." You'll eventually learn to love (or loathe) this word. But know that on your first day, your professor will either hand you a syllabus or tell you how you can find it online.

3. PROFESSORS ARE ALLOWED TO PONTIFICATE ABOUT ANYTHING THEY DEEM APPROPRIATE

In his first lecture on U.S. government, my professor for that class made a lot of things clear to the room full of students. He told us his views on politics, he shared with us that his wife liked calling him "doctor" during sex, and then he told us that under no circumstances were we to contradict his point of view in front of the class. "If you disagree with me on something, talk to me after class," he said.

Of course, not all teachers were this radical, and a lot of them were open to classroom discussion. However, many of them were quick to offer solid rebuttals to students' opinions. I quickly learned that, as long as their views were legal, college professors usually got away with talking about almost anything—which certainly made for a few *very* interesting lectures.

4. THANKSGIVING DAY IS A LONG WAY OFF

After eight hours of class on that first day, I counted the days until Thanksgiving—the school's first official break. For your own sanity, don't do this.

5. THE WORDS "I BELIEVE" ARE POWERFUL

I met many different people with many different worldviews on that first day. A few of those people would raise their hands and offer their own perspectives on what professors were communicating. They'd say, "I believe . . . ," and they'd offer their theories on politics, science, business, and the like. Once they were finished, the rest of the class would offer their opinions and views about those beliefs. Probably the most important thing I learned that day was to think before I spoke. Sure, I had opinions, and my opinions were important, just as important as everybody else's. But I realized that before I stood up in front of the class and said, "I believe . . . ," I needed to really know not only *what* I believed but also how to communicate it.

FOUR THINGS TO KNOW BEFORE YOU SAY, "I BELIEVE . . ."

1. People might judge you for what you believe.
2. People might create stereotypes about you because of what you believe.
3. People might not care about what you believe.
4. People might actually listen and respect your belief if it's communicated with love and compassion—they still might judge, create stereotypes, and not care, but love and compassion make our beliefs much easier for people to digest.

YOU CAN KISS YOUR FAMILY AND
FRIENDS GOOD-BYE AND PUT MILES
BETWEEN YOU, BUT AT THE SAME TIME
YOU CARRY THEM WITH YOU IN YOUR
HEART, YOUR MIND, YOUR STOMACH,
BECAUSE YOU DO NOT JUST LIVE IN A
WORLD BUT A WORLD LIVES IN YOU.

— FREDERICK BUECHNER

CHAPTER 1

GETTING READY

(Securing key relationships, writing a mission statement, seeing the big picture —yeah, so this is pretty much a chapter about all the stuff you should be doing instead of reading this book)

No period of my life has been one of such unmixed happiness as the four years which have been spent within college walls.
— HORATIO ALGER*

DESPITE WHAT YOU HAVE heard, getting ready for college is more than just signing up for classes, packing your belongings, and getting the heck out of Dodge. Well, at least, it should be more than signing, packing, and leaving. Depending on when you actually got this book, you either have a few weeks to get things completed or you have a couple of months. Either way, I want to add one more thing to your to-do list. I know what you're probably thinking: *I am too busy with a part-time job, friends, and college junk to add one more thing to my life.* Is that what you're thinking? Am I close? Did I ask the question too soon? I tend to do that sometimes.

Amid all the hustle of organizing a life away from home, you have got to consider the big picture—in other words, the BIG *change* that's coming. Yeah, so since you're going to college, one of the most important things you need to do is PREPARE. I know, I know—you hate preparation. But it's so important, like *Constitution of the United States*

---

* I don't know who the heck this guy is either, but I thought his quote was relevant.

important. But don't sweat it; I'm here to help you, remember? With me at your side, all the important stuff will surely get done. Of course, you'll still need a massage therapist when you're finished, 'cause it's not like I'm *really* there helping you pack, load the car, and set up your dorm room. (Ha ha ha ha! Sucker!)

Okay, getting back to the book. More than the supplies, the clothes, the class schedule, and all the other details that surround leaving for college, the big picture matters most. The big picture entails leaving all that you know as familiar—not just the geography but also your lifestyle, friends, community, and support. It's about you taking that giant step toward becoming an adult. Yes, even if you're living at home and attending a community college, a lot of that big-picture stuff still applies.

In a nutshell, the big picture is about you taking a stab at trying to see this college event from as many different perspectives as your life necessitates. Look at it from the perspective of your future. See it from the perspective of your friends at school and church. Try your darnedest to see it from your mom and dad's and siblings' perspectives. And most important, try to take a glance at it from God's perspective. Try to step out of your own little world and resist the temptation to make it all about you. For most of us, this is very difficult to do.

Let me tell you a secret. You might not be thinking about the big picture, but those you are leaving behind most definitely are. And more than likely, they're probably seeing only *their* big picture—your college career according to their own perspectives, which is what comes naturally for us as humans. Whether it's your mom and dad, a boyfriend or girlfriend, grandparents, brothers and sisters, or close relatives and friends, every important person in your life is probably anxiously dreading the day you make this life-changing leap. Sure, they are excited for you and desire nothing but the best for you and are probably putting up a really good front right about now. But they are also feeling the weight of what "you going to college" means for them. It's a transition for them, too, which is why it's important for you to try to view your next step from their perspectives, too.

Now, you might be thinking that all of this "perspectives stuff" sounds stupid or cheesy or overrated. Perhaps you think it's a little bit over the top. And for some of you, this might be right. Everybody's personal situation is different. Every college student has different hurdles to jump over in leaving the familiar; everyone has different feelings about what going away to college means. Some of you can hardly wait to be free of all that surrounds you. Others of you simply see the move to college as another step in life. And then there are some of you who are hoping it never comes — the thought of leaving Mom and Dad or your significant other or your friends scares you to death.

But no matter what category you fit into, God wants your college experience to be whole, which is why taking a moment to think about the big picture will help you and your loved ones be better prepared for what's to come. When you're selfless and reflective, God can open your eyes to see "the change" His way.

I promise, if you take the time to embrace the big picture a couple of months before you take the big leap into college, you will be readied, not only with your book bag, laundry detergent, and flip-flops, but more important, you will feel emotionally and spiritually grounded to tackle whatever college life hurls your way.

EMBRACING THE BIG PICTURE
(Because everyone needs to leave home with good relationships intact)

MAKE TIME FOR YOURSELF

In preparing for college, the best way to figure out what the big picture means for you is to get some time alone. Find a quiet spot, whether it's your bedroom or out in the forest or in the bathroom, sitting on the can. The place doesn't really matter; just make sure it's quiet and you're alone. Sorry, but public restrooms will probably not work for this exercise.

Quiet time, whether it's focused or not, is important throughout your life. But during the couple of months before college, quiet time lends itself nicely to helping you organize your thoughts, feel the weight of your upcoming move, and make wise decisions.

FACT:

I'm sure you've heard this before, but it seems fitting to mention it here again. Jesus, during His time on earth, took time for Himself. During these times He prayed, sought advice from His Father, and meditated. Getting time to yourself is a good habit to have for the rest of your life.

JOURNAL/BLOG ON LIFE

Most people try to avoid writing whenever possible. Believe me, as a full-time writer, I understand how just accomplishing my writing assignments is tough enough, let alone writing for leisure or reflection. But journaling or blogging your thoughts, prayers, and dreams a few times a week can really help clear your mind. Again, like a quiet time, this is a good habit to have throughout your life. But before college, journaling or blogging gives you a good opportunity to write down your fears, excitement, and quandaries about moving away, the change, and the new environment you will soon inhabit. You might write about the requests you've been asking God about. You might write a list of things you hope to accomplish your first year of school. You might write about how you believe your mom is handling your big move. No matter how you use it, keeping a journal or blog can help you focus your emotions on what is pure and true. And believe me, if you get homesick or frustrated or depressed while at college, being able to look back and read your thoughts from three or four months ago might help you through the harder times.

No doubt, those couple of months before leaving for college can create a lot of stress in a household. A lot of the students I have met often talk of a summer filled with arguments between them and their parents or unrest within dating relationships and friends. And a lot of students are feeling anxious about all that is going on around them. Believe me, all of this is quite normal. You're not the only one dealing with these kinds of pressures.

When trying to organize life before college, the mind can become cluttered, which leads to stress. More often than not, stress causes us to struggle with thinking healthily. When we think unhealthily, we tend to react harshly to the ones we love the most. But sometimes, when an individual has a hard time thinking with clarity of mind, he or she becomes breakdown-prone. And nobody wants to experience a breakdown. You've heard the horror stories about stress and breakdowns. Think Tara Reid. Courtney Love. Robert Downey Jr.* You've seen E! True Hollywood Story; you know about the drama that unhealthy stress can cause. And if you haven't, trust me; emotional breakdowns can be ugly.

Journaling and blogging certainly aren't foolproof. There's no guarantee that states, "Journaling will keep you from getting stressed." But journaling on a regular basis is a good way for the mind to unwind. It also allows some of the thoughts that fill your mind to be released. Even if no one else ever reads what you have written, the release of all that consumes your mind is good. And journaling or blogging are great ways for you to see not only yourself for who you are, but also the experience that you're about to encounter.

---

* Robert Downey Jr. used to be touted as one of the best actors in Hollywood, but alas, he failed to journal and consequently became addicted to heroin. See what happens when people don't journal? In case you're not getting the joke, I'm making all of this up. Well, at least, the journaling part.

FOUR STEPS TO JOURNALING

1. Find a journal, notebook, or blogging software.
2. Get some alone time; being alone is important.
3. Write down what your heart and mind are feeling; write down your prayers.
4. Remember, there are no set rules to journaling. Sometimes your thoughts might be funny or happy, and sometimes they might be angry or sad. Just write them down.

MAKE TIME FOR THE IMPORTANT PEOPLE IN YOUR LIFE

The people who are most influential in your life—the ones you love and cherish the most—are an important and necessary ingredient to your success while in college. Whether it's parents or grandparents or teachers or friends or youth pastors, their involvement in your university life is important. They are a part of the community that will help you remain grounded while at school. Scheduling time with them before you go will not only help you bring closure to those "immature days" of high school (oh, so long ago), but it will also give you the opportunity to tell those people about the influence they have had on your life. It also gives you an opportunity to stress your desire that they'll continue to be a reference in your life.

When you make time for the important people in your life, you're giving them a chance to bestow upon you their best advice. The wisdom of those you respect is important for the experience you're about to encounter.

PARENTS

For many of you, your parents are the people who have influenced you the most. Sure, your parents will be with you throughout your entire college experience (they may be helping you pay the bills, which certainly gives them a vested interest), but when I mention making *time* with them, I'm talking quality and not quantity. Schedule an afternoon with your father. Take your mom out on a date—just the two of you. Talk with them about their college experiences. Talk about how life is going to change. Let them cry a little about their "baby" being all grown up. Believe me, if you marry and have kids, you'll someday understand what they're feeling. This is *huge* for them. I know it feels cheesy and maybe a little awkward, but if you have a good relationship with your parents, this will be huge for you, too.

Let them give you their best and worst advice. If your parents share your faith, you might spend some time praying with them. Or you might simply drink iced soy lattes and talk about the weather, entertainment, or politics. In making time with your parents, you're giving them the chance to "let go," but more important, you're letting them know that you still need them. And no matter how much you might believe otherwise, you do need them. Whether you have the best parents in the world or ones who have long struggled to really be involved in your life, this simple act will let them know that you care.

SIBLINGS

If you have brothers or sisters who have gone away to college, then you know what it feels like when the house is suddenly void one person. For everyone it's a little different—some think of it as little more than a bad hair day, while for those who are a little more dramatic, it feels like a death.

I'm sure for some of you it was a joyous occasion when your older brother or sister finally left for school. You know who you are. Your desire to have your own bedroom overwhelmed the emotion inside to the point that you didn't feel anything at all. You were thinking only,

It's about time I got my own room! Well, if no one told you then, I'll tell you now: You were a selfish little brat!

Wow. That felt good. Just so you know, your siblings made me write that.

However, for most brothers and sisters, it's hard when one of the family members leaves the home. In fact, most of the time, it's pretty emotional for the sibling or siblings left behind with Mom and Dad. It certainly was for me when my two older sisters left for college. I was ten years old when my second-oldest sister left for college, and I cried for a couple of days after she left. Before she left, she took my little sister and me out for ice cream; that meant the world to us. It showed us that she cared about us.

So just like spending time with Mom and Dad is healthy for them and you, the same is true for your siblings. Even if you argue with your brother or sister like a dating pair fights on *The O.C.*, drop the feud long enough to spend an hour or two of quality time with them. Those couple of hours will go a long way toward possibly building a healthy relationship with the little guy or girl in the future. And remember, *they're so much more immature than you are.* (Yes, that was sarcasm.)

OTHERS

Usually, most future college students have other people in their lives—friends, grandparents, teachers, mentors, pastors, or counselors—who deserve time, too. This is especially true for those who don't have one or both parents still with them. Good people often come into our lives and fill voids left by tragedy, hard circumstances, or poor choices. These people are a part of the human network that helped you succeed during certain parts of your journey. They challenged you and directed you. They pushed you or lifted you up during the hard times.

You're probably thinking of two or three (maybe more) people right now who may or may not be related to you but whose godly wisdom, strong arms, and willingness to give of their time have had huge effects on your life. It's those kinds of people you want to keep with you when you enter this new journey of college. It's those people who will become your allies; they will sharpen you throughout your life at college and perhaps beyond.

So often, when we're really in trouble or when we've found ourselves in a situation that we never would have thought was possible, it's the youth pastors, counselors, and friends in our lives who first help us to pick up the pieces. It's not that our parents or siblings or grandparents don't care; it's just that sometimes it's not as easy to be open and honest with them. You might think that just because you're too old for the church youth group or have graduated from high school that those influential people have to be left in the past. But most often, this isn't the case.

A significant part of seeing the big picture is realizing that this college experience will require you to not leave the past behind, but to take the strong parts of your past with you.

The best advice I ever received was to surround myself with people smarter than myself. Realizing that this truth includes people at home as well as the new people you will meet is an important part of that advice.

Just remember that the people who have invested in you during your childhood and teenage years will probably be open to continuing their investment through your college experience. Engaging a deeper relationship with them almost always proves beneficial in the end.

WRITE A MISSION STATEMENT
(Because let's face it: You need a plan)

Okay, so this might sound a little crazy or too "adult" for you. You're probably thinking, *Most people don't think about their mission statement until they're out of college.* Sadly, you would be correct in that assumption. And truthfully, for many people, a personal mission statement *never* gets written. But I believe (as do many people smarter than me) that success greatly depends on an individual knowing where he or she wants to go in life. This doesn't mean you have to know what you're going to major in or where you want to work and live or how many kids you desire to have. But taking the time to write down a few sentences that detail what you're passionate about, what truly moves you, and what your deepest dreams entail often helps those other "bigger" decisions fall into place. Or, at least, it gives you a little direction. And it makes you seem a lot smarter than you probably are.

It's been proven over and over again that a large majority of the world's most successful people, whether they work in business, ministry, or service fields, have mission statements. And usually, the statement is not lengthy or dramatic; it's just three or four points that reveal the person's purpose and reason for being.

The mission statement you write today will probably change a little throughout college and could change drastically after college. College grows you in nearly every area of your life. Sometimes the growth experienced in college is good, but sometimes it just gets us off track from living out the plan God desires for our lives. That's why it's important to walk into the college life with a small (or big) idea of what you desire to get out of it. So in preparation for this big event in your life, jot down a few thoughts about what you want to do with the rest of your life.

PRACTICAL ADVICE ON WRITING A MISSION STATEMENT
(Because unless you're Stephen Covey's son or daughter, you don't know what you're doing—and that's cool)

Before you start writing a personal mission statement, you need to do a little homework. Yeah, I know; it's summer vacation and the thought of homework makes you almost as sick as hearing an Ashlee Simpson song on the radio, but work through it. You'll be fine.

1. WRITE DOWN YOUR SUCCESSES. These successes might come from home, school, sports, or a hobby. It doesn't really matter where you have found success; just write it down. Your successes help you realize what you're good at.

2. WRITE FOUR OF YOUR STRONGEST BELIEFS. These beliefs might be about your faith in God. They might be about family or friendships. They might be something your dad taught you. Just write down four statements about life that you believe to be true and that you consequently try to live out in your life.

3. WRITE DOWN YOUR GOALS. Dream as big as you want to. If you desire to be the next Ashton Kutcher—*what is his talent again?*—then write that down. If you want to run an orphanage in Romania, write that down, too. Whether it's about sports, peace, politics, marketing, fashion, entertainment, or faith, write down your goals. Gosh, do I have to over-explain everything?

4. WRITE YOUR PERSONAL MISSION STATEMENT. Now that you have a better understanding of what's important to you (based on the answers to those first three questions), write down three to four sentences that would define your personal mission in life. And remember, this will change. So don't try and make it perfect. But be honest. Upon completing your statement, share what you wrote with a couple of friends or your mom and dad; they can help you decide whether or not you have been truthful about yourself. And in some cases, they might encourage you to be more adventurous in your goals.

A SAMPLE MISSION STATEMENT

To find joy, fulfillment, and value in life, I will seek out opportunities at college to empower my heart, mind, and body. My core beliefs are centered on the Beatitudes of Jesus. I believe His teachings provide a framework for identifying, pursuing, and achieving the pleasures that last the longest and that are the most satisfying to humanity. For me, the greatest passion of all is being fully alive in Christ, receiving mercy and respect from family, friends, and other students.

– KATY BLASE, FRESHMAN

TALK TO GOD

(Because I'm not totally sure, but I think it's impossible to talk to God too much)

The concept of telling a Christian like yourself that you should talk to God about college seems rather elementary, I know. It's kind of like telling Madonna to make good music. Hmm, I'm not sure that analogy works. (I stare blankly at my computer screen for five minutes trying to think of a better comparison.) How about this? It's like telling a five-month-old puppy the 937th time to pee on the newspaper and not the rug. By the 937th time, you're convinced the puppy should know better. In fact, he *does* know better—he's peed in the right spot a number of times since you brought him home. But once in a while, he seemingly forgets and runs behind the couch and does his business there. In other words, until the puppy perfects the art of peeing on the newspaper, you have to keep telling him.

People are the same. The only difference is we never seem to perfect the art of including God in every aspect of our lives. And when we think we have, we've got a whole new set of problems to tend to. But that's a different book.

When I went to college, it was often easy for me to leave God out of life's equation. No matter how defined you believe your faith to be, expect growth and screwups while at college. In fact, sometimes growth and mistakes happen at the same time. No matter if you're attending a Christian college or a mainstream university, you'll more than likely be surrounded by new ideas, thoughts, people, and pleasures that will make you ask questions, experience fear, and eventually dive deeper into faith. It's easier than you might think to become so consumed with the new things of college life that you leave out personal time with the One who created you.

Throughout college, you'll go through moments when you feel close to God, but on the other hand college also brings about opportunities that will challenge your faith, provoke your beliefs, and leave you feeling far away from where you believe you should be. So in preparation for college, it's important to spend time talking to God. In fact, you can't talk to Him enough. And do yourself a favor; resist the temptation to simply talk to God in an effort to keep Him in the loop on your life. Instead, keep coming to Him and letting Him keep *you* in the loop.

Consequently, you might not pee behind the couch quite as often.

THREE VERSES FROM EPHESIANS 6 EVERY COLLEGE STUDENT SHOULD KNOW

So take everything the Master has set out for you, well-made weapons of the best materials. And put them to use so you will be able to stand up to everything the Devil throws your way. This is no afternoon athletic contest that we'll walk away from and forget about in a couple of hours. This is for keeps, a life-or-death fight to the finish against the Devil and all his angels.

Be prepared. You're up against far more than you can handle on your own. Take all the help you can get, every weapon God has issued, so that when it's all over but the shouting you'll still be on your feet. (verses 11-13)

HAVE A PARTY

(Basically, because parties are fun)

After you've finished packing, run to the mall for the hundredth time, and had your one-on-one times with all of those good people in your life, I think it's only fair to have a little fun before you hit the college grind. So text-message all of your friends and leave an away message up on IM with this info: "Going-away party at my house. It's going to be *hot*!" Of course, you might want to give them the date, time, and directions. And you should probably get your folks' permission on this one before you do it. And then, with everyone you love the most surrounding you, party like it's 1999—oh, wait, that's what I did. Party like it's 2020.

OKAY, NOW FOR THE PRACTICAL GETTING-READY JUNK

(The part of the college preparation chapter you might already know, but go ahead and read it anyway—if nothing else, it might be a little entertaining)

TWENTY-SIX THINGS
you probably need to do before you leave for college

[ ] 1. GO VISIT YOUR COLLEGE. It's rare that one attends a college without ever having visited it. What if the school simply had a good photographer? What if the campus smells? What if the janitors don't do good work? Attending a college you've never visited is kind of like being in love with a woman you've seen only in the movies. It's like I once felt about Halle Berry. In some instances, for those of you who are moving as far away from your hometown as you can get, visiting your college may be impossible. But if it's an option, it's always a good one.

[ ] 2. REGISTER FOR CLASSES. Some colleges offer early registration times during the summer. I highly recommend you take advantage of this if it's available at your school. Also, most colleges offer online registration. Either way, register for classes as early in the summer as possible. Trust me; you *want* to beat the rush. Icky feelings prevail in long registration lines. Plus, if you beat the rush, you choose the schedule you want. If, on the other hand, you wait until the last minute, I guarantee you'll be stuck with the dreaded 8 a.m. and 5 p.m. classes.

I recommend you call your university and try to get in touch with your advisor (every student has one). He or she can help you figure out the best schedule for you.

[ ] 3. DOUBLE-CHECK THE **STATUS** OF **YOUR SCHOLARSHIPS, GRANTS, AND LOANS**. Quadruple-check the status, as it will make you feel better. Loan officers are about as accurate as the local weatherman. Sure, you believed the guy when he told you last month that everything was prepped and ready to go, but who's it going to hurt if you call again? And when you do, tell Henry at the loan office to e-mail you all the necessary information right away. If all ends up kaput when you're standing in the financial aid line, having all of the documents with you in writing will make you feel better and will make the uninterested loan office employees feel more obliged to help you. In fact, it pretty much makes you *the man*. Unless you're a woman. Then it makes you a mean-spirited soul in need of salvation. I'm not sure why it works that way, but it does.

[ ] 4. PURCHASE **YOUR PLANE TICKET**. If your parents think you're going too darn far away from home for college, then you're probably planning on flying to college. Well, begin looking for the best airline prices in June. Check out Expedia.com (they're the ones who sing "Dot Com" with a little country flair) or Travelocity.com (they don't have any catchy tune to help you remember) for competitive rates. But also check out Southwest.com (basically, an uncomfortable city bus with wings) because Southwest's rates do not show up on Expedia and Travelocity. Also, sign up for an airline awards plan and then try to fly that airline every time you come home. You might as well try to earn a free spring break flight.

[ ] 5. ASK **YOUR COLLEGE ABOUT DORM ROOM SIZE AND STORAGE SPACE**. Ha ha ha ha . . . I don't know why this one makes me laugh. Perhaps it's because most dorm rooms are just a little bit bigger than a Nerds candy container. Again, if you're not able to visit your college and see the dorm rooms for yourself, you will definitely want to find out from

the housing department the size of your room and how much closet space will be available to you. Ha ha ha ha ha . . . sorry, can't stop laughing. And whatever you do, don't expect to like the answer. In fact, before you even pick up the phone to call, go ahead and feel frustrated and deflated. Here are some ideas of how you can fit all your stuff in:

- Buy two large under-the-bed storage containers; you'll be able to fit all kinds of things in them—magazines, books, ex-love letters, a can opener, and two plush snowmen. Of course, other things, too.
- Get a hanging door organizer for shoes, hair supplies, and Skittles—lots of Skittles. Taste the rainbow.
- Leave the fifteen crates at home; what they have in storage capacity they lack big-time in flexibility.
- Bring seven pairs of large white socks—the largest socks you can find. Then, play a game with yourself and see if you can figure out why on earth I would suggest bringing along seven pairs of large socks.
- Buy an iPod; leave the CD collection HOME!

[ ] 6. WHILE YOU'RE AT IT, ASK WHAT YOUR DORM COMES WITH, TOO. Some colleges provide Frodo-sized refrigerators and other pointless small appliances. Find out if your school is one of them.

[ ] 7. FIND OUT IF THE MATTRESS IN YOUR ROOM IS LONG OR EXTRALONG. Yep, who knew that twin mattresses came in two different sizes? Can anyone tell me why? Oh, by the way, you'll need this information before you purchase bedding and sheets.

[ ] 8. BUY GOOD LUGGAGE. Hopefully, someone you know who has a lot of money thought about purchasing you a good set of luggage as a graduation gift. But if not, you will want to take out a second mortgage on your parents' home and buy some luggage. And if there's not a huge price difference, always go with the better brand. Sturdy luggage will last you a long time. You might check sites like eBay, too.

[ ] **9. GET YOUR IMMUNIZATIONS.** Check with your college on what shots are required because in rare cases, some states' and colleges' expectations differ from each other. *Big surprise there, huh?* Also, if you're going international, get your immunizations in early June. Depending on where you are going and what types of shots you need, some immunizations require a second visit.

[ ] **10. LEARN YOUR COLLEGE TOWN'S CLIMATE IF YOU DON'T ALREADY KNOW IT.** Usually the college will offer this information, but if not, you can check a town's average temperatures, rain, and snowfall and normal heat index at Weather.com. You'll want this information before you go shopping.

[ ] **11. CHECK TO SEE IF YOUR SCHOOL HAS A DRESS CODE.** Some Christian schools (and a couple Ivy League schools) require students to dress in a certain manner during classes. In fact, some Christian schools require you to dress a certain way any time you're around "mixed" company. Be sure you know what to expect. Those of you going to state colleges or universities need not pay any attention to this item on the list. (Good for you! You now only have twenty-five things to do.)

[ ] **12. VISIT YOUR DOCTOR, DENTIST, AND EYE DOCTOR.** It's good to get all of this medical stuff out of the way all at once while you're still at home. You don't want some *strange* doctor grabbing the intimate areas of your anatomy and asking you to cough. So get it done when you're still at home.

[ ] **13. LET'S TALK MEDS.** If you are taking any daily medications, make sure you ask your doctor to give you a prescription that will last you at least one full semester. Also, if you have any special medical needs, make sure the college is aware of your situation at least two months before you show up.

[ ] 14. MORE INFO ABOUT PRESCRIPTION MEDICATIONS. If you're on medication for depression, ADHD, anxiety, obsessive-compulsive disorder, or any other type of psychological or mental health condition, be sure to have a copy of your written prescription in a safe place in your dorm room at all times. And keep the meds in their original bottles. This precaution is just in case your roommate gets busted on possessions charges. (If you don't have your prescription, these kinds of meds could actually be confiscated. But that's likely to happen only if your roommate has pot in your room. Your original container proves that the meds are legit.)

[ ] 15. CHECK YOUR SCHOOL ABOUT ITS RULE REGARDING BIRTH CONTROL. At some Christian colleges, taking birth control is against the school policy. So for the ladies who are on a form of birth control to maintain a regular period or for any other physical reason (other than for protection against pregnancy), you will want to check with your particular school to set up the necessary arrangements in order for you to keep on your regimen. Although this is a rare situation, I promise I'm not making this up.

[ ] 16. TALK TO YOUR EMPLOYER ABOUT YOUR LAST DAY OF WORK. I'm pretty sure your employer is probably aware that you're not planning on making a career out of being a restaurant server, merchandise salesman, or carpenter assistant. So go ahead and break the "leaving" news to him as soon as you know, and give a specific end date. Also, offer to do any extra work he may desire of you before you go. This will leave him with a good impression of you, and that means there's a better chance that he'll let you come back to work over school breaks and the summer holiday. But if you hate the job, by all means, avoid *ever* going back.

[ ] 17. LET THE POSTAL SERVICE KNOW ABOUT YOUR CHANGE IN ADDRESS. Do this at least ten days before leaving so you divas won't miss out on *ELLEgirl*, you jocks won't miss out on *ESPN*, and you geeks won't miss out on *Wired*. Of course, that change in address will also ensure that your cell phone bill, credit card statement, and all the junk mail you will ever want will get forwarded, too. Also, for all the mail that really matters, make sure you contact each vendor individually to make a permanent change to your address.

[ ] 18. GET YOUR CAR'S OIL CHANGED. If you're lucky enough to have your own transportation, remind your dad that you'd like it serviced before you go away to school. Just tell him you don't do Midas.

[ ] 19. GET THE BOOK LIST FOR YOUR CLASSES EARLY (IF AVAILABLE). See your school's website or check with your campus bookstore to find out the names of the books you will need for your first semester. Get this list as early as possible and buy as many of them as you can online at Amazon, eBay, Overstock, or Half.com. This will save you tons of money because your campus bookstore will unabashedly rip you off.

[ ] 20. CALL YOUR FUTURE ROOMMATE(S). Connecting with your room-mate before you shack up with him or her inside that Nerds container for a year is a really good idea. On top of saying hello, find out what stuff—TV, dorm furniture, DVD player, video game equipment, and other larger dorm necessities—your roommate will be bringing with him or her. Try to get to know him or her a little bit and discover what you have in common—and what you don't—so you can be prepared.

[ ] 21. GET A LIST OF YOUR COLLEGE'S NONAPPROVED DORM ITEMS. Some colleges allow microwave ovens in dorms; some do not. Some colleges allow candles, tea lights, and heated potpourri; some don't. Appliances that have hot surfaces or heating elements inside, like toast-ers, hot plates, and coffeemakers, usually come into question, too. Before you buy any questionable appliance or load anything into your car, know what your college will and won't allow.

[ ] 22. GET AN INSURANCE CARD. More than likely you'll be on your parents' health insurance policy. Be sure your parents get your own personal card printed in case of emergencies. And if they refuse, threaten to make out with the first person you know who has mono.

[ ] 23. SET UP A BANK ACCOUNT. A lot of students set up their bank accounts the week classes begin. But if you know what banks are available around your college, why not get this little inconvenience out of the way during the summer? It's not like you're going to have that much money in there anyway. But having a bank account will at least ensure that you will be able to get those twenty-dollar checks from Grandma cashed. You gotta love Grandma!

[ ] 24. PLANNING ON GOING GREEK? EARLY APPLICATION PROCESS IS AVAILABLE AT SOME SCHOOLS. Certain sororities and fraternities offer students the chance to apply early. Check with your school's Greek program for more information.

[ ] 25. FIND A CHURCH. RelevantMagazine.com, as well as other websites, allow you to look up churches in many areas across the United States. If you aren't familiar with your college's town, it might be to your advantage to find out information about churches that are near your school. Check out the church's website, and try to find out about possible Bible studies, ministry opportunities, and whether the church offers transportation to and from campus.

[ ] 26. FIND OUT ABOUT LOCAL PUBLIC TRANSPORTATION. If you're not able to take a car to school, and if you hate the idea of riding a bicycle around campus, and if the concept of walking sixty-two miles across grounds for a 7 a.m. class makes you weary, call your college's student services center to get all the information and costs associated with the public transportation available on or around your campus. Also, ask your university if they provide bus passes to students. Usually only state schools make this kind of offer available, but why not ask? Who's it going to hurt? Only if the person you ask is violently against those who ask about free bus passes would I even think about worrying. So you're golden.

Okay, so the car is packed, you're partied out, and you feel prepped emotionally for the big leap into college life. And even if you're not *completely* packed, partied, and prepped, you'll be okay. You might not have gotten this book in time to do *everything* right. So no matter if you're feeling chaotic, numb, constipated, or content as you prepare to leave for college, just remember that you're not alone in this feeling. Not only are thousands of college students all over the world feeling similar emotions as you, but also know that God is walking with you through this change.

And if it means anything, I think you're going to be very success-ful. *And I don't even know you.* I mean, if *I* think that, what must your parents think?

THE CONCLUDING LIST

Write these five things from this chapter on a piece of paper and then eat it.

1. JOURNAL! You're either going to hate me for bringing this up again or proclaim your allegiance to journaling. Whichever you decide, journal about it.

2. WRITE A MISSION STATEMENT. This will give you a good sense of direction as you prepare to begin college.

3. VISIT YOUR CAMPUS. Or at least make sure you've seen some *very* good pictures.

4. SPEND GOOD MONEY ON A GOOD BACKPACK. If you're a girl, your boyfriend will thank me when he's dragging your "burden" to class. If you're a boy, you will thank me because at least *one* of the book bags you're carrying is a good one.

5. TALK TO GOD. Live the kind of life that never lets the conversation stop.

WHAT GREATER THING IS THERE FOR HUMAN
SOULS THAN TO FEEL THAT THEY ARE
JOINED FOR LIFE — TO BE WITH EACH OTHER
IN SILENT UNSPEAKABLE MEMORIES.

— GEORGE ELIOT

CHAPTER 2

RELATIONSHIPS

(Getting along with people is a must, so buy some tic tacs, wash your hair, and go meet some friends!)

You have four years to be irresponsible here. Relax. Work is for people with jobs. You'll never remember class time, but you'll remember time you wasted hanging out with your friends. So stay out late. Go out on a Tuesday with your friends when you have a paper due Wednesday. The work never ends, but college does.

— TOM PETTY*

ROCK 'N' ROLL LEGEND Tom Petty makes an interesting point in his advice to college students. In fact, if I hadn't needed to edit out his rather poor counsel to *go out and drink until the sun comes up* and to *spend every bit of the money that you don't have*, I might have forgotten the fact that Tom was rumored to have struggled with alcohol abuse many years ago and actually filed for bankruptcy once in his career. I guess some people don't like it when others learn from their mistakes.

However, I still liked Tom's quote. His encouragement for college students to focus on the relational aspect of college is indeed wisdom. Despite his words being laced with pop-cultural religion, which preaches the belief that life is about living for almighty *me*, Tom's

---

* On top of being a rather wise counselor on seeking out relationships, Tom Petty, along with his band The Heartbreakers, have also made some of the best rock 'n' roll around. If you like thought-provoking songs with a tendency to rock, check out his music at iTunes. I recommend *Into the Great Wide Open*, the band's 1991 release.

overall message, that the time spent building relationships is what you eventually will take with you, is indeed true.

EXTRA ADVICE FOR LONG-LASTING RELATIONSHIPS

Invest in a large supply of mints and/or gum. As we all have experienced, nothing is more offensive *or more memorable* to a first-time meeting than when a new acquaintance suffocates you with his foul breath. You don't want to be *that* guy, do you?

What you will likely remember most about college is the relationships you create. Sure, college is about getting an education, getting a good start on the rest of your life, and figuring out who you are. But the relationships (both the good ones and the bad) that you create during the years spent at college will be more influential to you than the classes you take, the knowledge you gain, and the trades you learn.

No matter if you refer to it as community, fellowship, friendship, or companionship, it's been proven over and over again in countless studies done by people more intelligent than me that humans are healthier when surrounded by the support of good relationships. (Not to mention the fact that the Bible makes a clear case for the need for relationship.) If you were to speak to every psychologist, pastor, and philosopher in the world, most of them would tell you that good relationships with other people are some of the most important ingredients to an individual's happy and healthy lifestyle. Can we *live* without relationships? Sure we can. But usually, a person without good relationships lives only physically. His emotional life goes crazy.

As a result of this basic human need, true success, the kind of success that really means something in the end, is based on your ability to build good relationships. You'll find this to be true throughout your life and not just on a campus for four years. As you just finished reading in chapter 1, much of the big picture that I wrote about focused on defining, securing, and cherishing those relationships you already have in your life right now. The bond that you share with your family, friends, mentors, and God will become the foundation for creating good relationships during your time at college. If you have strong relational foundations, they will become the jumping-off points for the relationships you will make in school. And if you don't, college offers a chance to begin anew.

So as you get ready to leave—or if you're already living there and trying to get settled in—know this to be true: Good relationships will help you succeed. And unlike the friends and mentors you developed in high school and the love you have within your family, the community you build at college will be your first opportunity as a newly christened "adult" to try out your personal people skills on *other* freshly christened "adults."

FOUR VERSES FROM MATTHEW 5 THAT EVERY COLLEGE STUDENT SHOULD KNOW

"Let me tell you why you are here. You're here to be salt-seasoning that brings out the God-flavors of this earth. If you lose your saltiness, how will people taste godliness? You've lost your usefulness and will end up in the garbage.

"Here's another way to put it: You're here to be light, bringing out the God-colors in the world. God is not a secret to be kept. We're going public with this, as public as a city on a hill. If I make you light-bearers, you don't think I'm going to hide you under a bucket, do you? I'm putting you on a light stand. Now that I've put you there on a hilltop, on a light stand – shine! Keep open house; be generous with your lives. By opening up to others, you'll prompt people to open up with God, this generous Father in heaven." (verses 13-16)

For some of you, relationship building comes easy—you're outgoing, easy to talk to, and outwardly friendly. But for some, the art of making friends feels awkward and unnatural. You'd rather do almost anything than talk to a stranger. What you might find interesting is that people on both sides of the extrovert/introvert fence are prone to struggle with building healthy relationships.* Why? Because building good relationships is much more than being quick and comfortable at saying, "Hi, how are you?" In other words, it's not always the relationship part that's the hardest struggle; the *healthy* part is what gives most of us grief. Quite often our college experience brings to the surface the personality inconsistencies that make good relationships harder.

But I don't believe you're powerless in your relationship woes. I believe you can prepare yourself for the "relational journey" of college. Building good relationships is more than simply following a few clichéd rules, like don't make a complete *donkey* of yourself, refrain from acting like you know *everything*, and my personal favorite, be nice to them and they'll be nice to *you*. I hate to break it to you, but although these rules are brilliant and should be followed, unfortunately, following them doesn't ensure good relationships. In fact, whoever made up the "be nice to them and they'll be nice to you" statement must not have hung around too many people; he was either a recluse monk or a publicly veiled offspring of Michael Jackson. Furthermore, hanging around *people* for any length of time would result in even the most moronic person realizing that *being nice* doesn't secure kindness in return. I wish it did. Okay, I know that's a little over-the-top, but it's genuinely true. And if you can't tell by now, I like a little drama.

So I don't want to make relationship building sound like rocket science, but you should know that your relational journey will last a lifetime. As you know, this college experience is about growing.

---

* Yes, I realize that in categorizing an individual into either an "easy" column or a "hard" column greatly simplifies the issue of building relationships. But cut a guy some slack; I have only so many words to work with in this book. And using the introvert/extrovert theory seemed to me to be the easiest way to get my point across.

Nobody expects you to be perfect. And though some of the relationship building in college is difficult, most of the people you meet in college will change your life for the better.

BASIC TIPS ON FINDING CHRISTIAN FRIENDS ON ANY CAMPUS

Okay, so I don't want to give the impression that I believe it's good to create relationships with Christians only, because I wholeheartedly disagree with that logic. It's clear that as Christians we are called to interact with people who don't know Jesus in order to introduce them to Him. But I also believe that relationships with people who share your faith will be important to you. In fact, I would even venture to say that, for some of you, these might be the most important kinds of relationships that you will need when you're at college. On certain campuses it's simple to find Christian relationships, but the same cannot be said for all schools. If you're at a loss for where to begin, here are a few ideas to help you get connected with other Christians. (And, yes, they're pretty basic.)

- JOIN CAMPUS COLLEGE MINISTRIES. Many colleges have faith-based groups that meet weekly. The most common groups are Navigators, Campus Crusade for Christ, Fellowship of Christian Athletes, InterVarsity, the Catholic Student Union, and the Baptist Student Union. If your college has more than one of the above (and if you live in the South, it probably does), visit all of the groups at least once. (I'll write more about campus ministries later in the book.) But either way, these groups are a great way to get connected.

- VISIT LOCAL CHURCHES. I think this is pretty self-explanatory unless you're really slow. But know this: Some churches adjacent to your college might have young-adult church services you can attend or college ministries where you can get involved.

- DON'T BE AFRAID TO VISIT ANOTHER COLLEGE'S MINISTRY. This idea might be a little hard for some of you, but I still think it's a good one. If your college offers no campus ministry or church-led Christian study, there might be another school in the area that does. Contact that school's ministry leader. Most college ministries are open to having students from other schools be a part of their weekly groups.

- TRY MYSPACE.COM. Websites like MySpace and Friendster or Facebook are also great resources to use for finding other Christian students at your school.

- WEAR A JESUS T-SHIRT AROUND CAMPUS. And that way, all of the Christians will come to you. *I'm kidding.* No, I really am. However, carrying around a copy of Donald Miller's *Blue Like Jazz* might work even better these days, and it's a little more covert than wearing "CK: Christ Is King" across your chest. But between you and me, I'll probably label "carrying around *Blue Like Jazz*" uncool in a couple of years, too.

- SPEAK UP. Just by talking to many different people, you might be surprised how often you'll meet someone who shares your love of Jesus. Just don't be weird or offensive about it. You know what I mean.

RELATIONSHIP 101: PURSUING A RELATIONAL LIFESTYLE

(Because you will be very bored and lonely if you don't have good relationships)

- -

FOCUSING ON THE PROBABLE CORE OF
ALL OF YOUR RELATIONSHIP PROBLEMS — *YOU*

(Because despite this not always being true, it's probably more true than you're willing to admit. And that problem with "admitting" might be your first problem. This has to be longest subtitle in a book ever.)

A few years ago, I befriended a girl named January. Yes, *January*. For some reason, that name strikes me as odd. And honestly, to this day, I don't believe her name is *really* January. But when I met her, she refused to admit otherwise. A parent naming a child after any of the twelve months except April, May, June, and an occasional August seems to be cruel and unusual. So maybe I'm narrow-minded on this one. Whatever.

When I met the then twenty-one-year-old, she was just beginning her junior year at a university in Northern Virginia. As she sat down at one of the bar stools at the coffeehouse where I worked, I could tell something was bothering her. Her face looked flush from crying and one lonely tear was still making its way down one side of her cheek. She ordered an iced mocha latte with two shots of espresso. Being rather outgoing and fearless around people (sometimes to a fault), I asked her how life was treating her.

"It's okay, I guess," she said with a slight frown.

"You don't seem too sure about that," I said. She laughed a little but didn't immediately elaborate on what was bothering her. Before long, we were engaged in conversation.

January was a plain-looking girl; her hair was long and dark, and her eyes were almost black, but it was her skin tone that caught my attention. Because of what she referred to as "my mother's good Syrian genes," her complexion was near perfect. I watched her as she stirred six Equals into her drink. While she sipped her chilled latte, I cleaned up behind the counter and took care of the occasional customer. For more than thirty minutes, January and I chatted off and on about everything from the weather to her college's pathetic basketball team to my disbelief that her name was *really* January. But eventually, the conversation took a more serious turn.

"Can I ask you a question?" she asked slowly, seeming rather hesitant.

Instantly, because of her tone, I knew that her question was going to relate to why she had been crying. And suddenly, I kind of felt like one of those clichéd, overly concerned bartenders that Hollywood likes to put in the movies. Of course, the only difference was that January was drowning her sorrows in a plastic cup filled with strong faux-sweetened coffee and not in a drink with a lot of Grey Goose mixed in.

"Sure, I like questions," I said.

"I need to talk to someone about what's going on in my life," she explained. "And you seem like a normal enough stranger."

"That comment is supposed to be a compliment, right?" I said, grinning again slightly.

"Yes!"

"Good, I'll take it that way."

"Do you have many close friends?"

"I have a few more than enough."

January looked at me again, with a serious look on her face. "You know, I have been going to college for just a little over two years here in Fairfax County, and I don't have one friend. At least, I don't have a good friend. Not one. Honestly, I'm not even sure why I came back this semester other than the fact that my mother made me return, and to be honest, life's not *that* much better back in New York."

January looked down into her coffee as she spilled her guts. It was almost as if I wasn't there; January didn't look at me too often.

"I'm beginning to think something is seriously wrong with me," she said.

Despite feeling a little awkward about how quickly the conversation had gone from my saying how bad her college's basketball team was to her telling me that she had no friends, I listened intently to her story.

With the detail of a Dickens novel, January explained how, since she was in seventh grade, she had struggled to make friends. For most of her middle-school and high-school life, she had been the target of overconfident jocks and bullies and the mockery of girls who were cheerleaders. Once in a while, even her father would tell her that she needed to lose a little weight.

"For some reason, despite being out of that kind of environment for nearly three years, I still struggle letting anyone get too close to me. I'm still suffering from the pain I felt so many years ago."

Listening to this young woman's story, I quickly realized that a seventy-five-minute conversation with me, a mere coffeehouse barista, was not going to do her any good; she needed some type of counseling to overcome her insecurities with people. January's issues with relationships were deeply rooted in a great deal of pain. It was obvious to me that she was still letting her past define who she was to other people. And as far as I could tell, the person January was seeing when she looked in the mirror was someone she didn't like. In fact, it's not too much of a stretch to say that she didn't even know the girl she saw in the mirror. To January, all people saw when they looked at her was an overweight girl with no friends. Unfortunately, as has been the case with a lot of people, January's college life had brought a lot of buried pain and frustrations to the surface. It wasn't other people January struggled with; it was herself she was fighting.*

Perhaps you can't entirely relate to January's story, but I bet you can at least relate to having difficult experiences relating to others. We've all been teased or ridiculed and have struggled with personal issues like weight, acne, or things even more personal. But the real truth here is this: You have to know *you*. When someone doesn't know

---

* I saw January three other times after that first meeting. Toward the end of her junior year, she finally decided to seek out the help of a Christian counselor. The last time I heard from her, January had graduated from college and was involved in her first *real* dating relationship. But according to her, life got harder before it got easier.

who he is, relationships become much harder because it's difficult to let other people become close to you when you're not comfortable in your own skin. Insecurities often become so overwhelming to this kind of person that relationships with others tend to short-circuit.

It's hard to see what we look like to other people when we fail to take the time to look in the "mirror" ourselves. When I went to college, several of my relationships suffered from my inability to see myself for who I really was; I failed to see my own shortcomings with selfishness, obnoxious behavior, and the urge to focus too much attention on being "controversial."

Attempting to know *you* is an important task before you go to college. So get ready to take a long look in the mirror. For you to create healthy relationships that sharpen you to be all you can be, it's imperative that you recognize all of the good and bad that your personality brings into the room. This exercise won't make you perfect in relating to people, but recognizing your flaws and strengths is the first step.

FOUR BASIC TIPS TO MAKING STRONG CONNECTIONS WITH PEOPLE

1. FIRST THINGS FIRST: TALK TO GOD. Ask God to really show you how people view *who* you are and let Him make some changes in your life. (I'll talk a lot about this in the next section of this chapter.) Often we humans can be pretty stupid. We think it's possible to hide our flaws and mask how those flaws make our relationships suffer. Instead of hiding, we need to be dealing with the problem(s). No one can forever hide anger or negativity or neediness when they're at college. It's almost impossible. And frankly, you don't want to hold on to that junk anyway. It's important to get to the root of why you act a certain way around people, and then, ask God to help you work through these problems. This is important not only for college, but also for the rest of your life.

2. BEGIN SLOWLY AND LET A RELATIONSHIP GROW. Okay, I'm just going to say it. Nobody likes someone who is trying to force a friendship. In many cases, these kinds of people have "potential stalker" written all over them.

Remember, when you're at college, everyone you meet those first few weeks is going to be in the same boat as you are – looking for a way to connect with people. Honestly, it's a really lonely time, but you'll get through it. At first, there are a thousand or more possibilities for friendships. So, knowing you have many options, try approaching friendships slowly with a little bit of good tact. This way, you're giving people a chance to truly see the gift of a person you really are, and you'll make natural connections that last. But more important, these connections will be real and honest; they won't be friendships that other people will see as forced or manipulated.

3. THE SINCERITY TO KNOW SOMEONE'S STORY GOES A LONG WAY. Strong connections are often built through a sincere desire to get to know someone. In other words, don't make the first conversation with a person all about you. Self-centeredness stinks like a men's locker room. (And for you girls who have never smelled a men's locker room, trust me, it can get pretty ripe.) Instead of monopolizing the time talking about yourself, ask questions. Of course, don't ask *too-personal* questions – you're not Dr. Phil – just ask your basic questions about a person's hometown, college major, hobbies, and future dreams. If you have a connection, feel free to go deeper! Trust me, you'll know pretty quickly if you click (unless you're one of those people whose first impressions are always wrong . . . in that case, give it a little more time).

4. EXPECT TO BECOME FRIENDS WITH PEOPLE WITH WHOM YOU DON'T HAVE MUCH IN COMMON. Some people say that it's good to always build on your commonalities with others, and to a point, that's a good theory. But in college, that doesn't always work, and actually, it would be a shame to only befriend people like you. You're going to meet people from different backgrounds, with different philosophies and ideas. But don't run from diversity. Instead, build on it. We Christians are too often guilty of grouping ourselves together and ignoring others, but now that you're an adult, you can use differences as opportunities to learn new ideas and be challenged by other worldviews.

YOU GETTING TO KNOW YOU
(Why? Because you are great! You are fabulous! You are successful. And because you NEED FRIENDS!)

Okay, so remember that journal you started back in chapter 1? Go get it. You'll need it for this next section.

I realize that probably a good percentage of you are just *reading* this book and might be avoiding the extracurricular "assignments" at all costs. But if you are one of the few who actually *want* to get something out of this book, please grab that journal and pen. (I'll wait here until you get back.)

Those of you who are moving right now are officially my new favorites. And as for the rest of you nonmoving, lazy college students, this new relationship that you and I have begun is starting to suffer by your lack of involvement. Please don't make me get needy. Because, believe me, I can.

How about this idea? Why not write your thoughts to this next section in the space provided, and if you need more space, in the margins of this book?

If that would actually get you to participate, then by all means, use the margins.

Okay, now back to "you getting to know *you*."

Remember, getting to know you "the package" is not a one-time gig. It's an ongoing process that you should pursue your entire life. Making an ongoing effort to see yourself as others see you and ultimately how God sees you will hopefully enable you to begin to see the need for a few changes, but it will also give you the opportunity to notice the parts of you that are most physically, emotionally, and spiritually attractive to others. Looking in the "mirror" on a regular basis will also help you know what God desires to see come out of your life.

Use the following questions to help you journal. If you find the questions in any way limiting or formulaic, then please, simply journal about "how well you know yourself" on your own. These questions are here only to help you get started.

- Write down five personal strengths that you demonstrate in relationships.
- How do these strengths help you get to know people, keep friendships, and define the friends you'll pursue?
- Would your best friend disagree with you on any of the traits that you listed as strengths? How about your parents? Your employer?

- Has there ever been a situation where your strengths have been a weakness in relationships? In other words, many times our greatest strengths are also our greatest weaknesses. Is this true for you? And if it's true, how so?
- What part of your personality or story do people first encounter when they meet you? Is it kindness? Peacefulness? Is it your sense of humor? Or is it something more obnoxious? Perhaps it's a political or spiritual view? Or maybe it's how you dress.
- Write down five personal flaws that you demonstrate in relationships.
- How do these flaws hinder you in relationships? Do they make you seem codependent? Needy? Over-the-top? Judgmental? Selfish?

Writing down how you see yourself is only the beginning of knowing what you bring into the room with you when you meet new people. But to begin this process now is not only healthy and at times freeing; you'll notice your friendships being stronger and more real. And who doesn't want that?

THE TRUTH ABOUT ROOMMATES

The idea of living in a tiny room with someone you don't know can be a little overwhelming. Many college students have all kinds of thoughts and fears about living with a roommate for the first time. In fact, as I was writing this book, I asked a few former college students if they remembered their first thoughts about having a roommate. Nearly every one of them had some reservations at first.

Here's a sample of the thoughts and questions they had beforehand:

- What if he's weird?
- What if she has disgusting personal habits?
- What if she ends up being psychotic?
- What if he uses drugs?
- Do you think he'll have sex with his girlfriend when I'm in the room?

○ What if she's crazy; I mean, *really crazy*?

○ What if he farts a lot?

While the occasional crazy, oversexed, overgassed roommate certainly exists, more than likely your roommate will be someone you can bear living with for a year or two, and your roommate may even become a good friend you'll stay in touch with throughout your life. Anything can happen. Who knows, you may be the unlucky sap who ends up with a horrible roommate. But remember: You can transfer. You need but a semester to decide whether you can hack it with your roommate or not, and if you just can't, request a transfer. It's likely you'll have made a new friend you'd rather live with, but since very few colleges are opposed to students' happiness, they're likely to grant your request if you want to change.

If you haven't planned ahead of time to live with someone you know from high school or church, your school will likely send you a letter with your roommate's name and contact information. When you get this letter, send your roommate a letter or give him or her a call. If possible, set up a date and place to meet. By communicating before move-in day, a lot of your questions and concerns will be answered. But often, connecting with your roommate is difficult. So if this doesn't happen, don't get frustrated. Most likely your roommate will be *nothing* like that crazy girl from the movie *SwimFan*, but I guess you never know until you get to know him or her, huh? (Am I making you feel any better? I'm *really* trying.)

One thing that is good to remember: Your roommate is probably just as worried about you. He doesn't know if you're a nutcase, either, and is probably also a little nervous that you are going to be super weird or someone he can't relate to, or maybe he's scared you might be someone who ends up becoming attracted to him. All kinds of crazy things go through people's heads when they think about their future roommate. So if possible, definitely communicate ahead of time with him or her. This will simply allow you both to get to know at least some surface information about each other. But you won't know everything, so follow this advice and you and your roommate(s) will get along fine (probably).

HELPFUL HINTS FOR HAPPY ROOMMATING

(Advice! Advice! Advice is so NICE! If you follow these rules, you won't be a fool, and no one will ever call you a tool!)

- **HAVE A CONVERSATION ABOUT CLEANLINESS.** If both of you are slobs, then great. But if one of you lives like King Kong and the other like Martha Stewart, your dorm life happiness will depend on your working through this fundamental difference. Do yourself a huge favor and talk about this ahead of time. And most important, be honest about your personal housekeeping habits, and be willing to make compromises.

- **ONLY SHARE THE BIG STUFF.** On the front end, it *seems* like the perfect concept: two new roommates willing to share everything from the flatscreen TV to the hair dryer to the expensive hair gel to even the occasional shirt or coat or shoes. But in the long run (and you can trust me on this one), just share things like the TV, a microwave, and stereo. And perhaps, *after* you've seen your roommate's good handling of all her things, *then* let her borrow your coat. But proceed with caution! I know that giving freely is good (we'll talk about that later), but unless you have a high tolerance for being annoyed or you are looking to gain the patience of Mother Teresa, then think before you allow your roomie to borrow your stuff.

- **IF IT FEELS GOOD, *DO IT*. BECOME FRIENDS, THAT IS.** You might discover that you and your roommate get along splendidly. And if that's the case, go ahead and be the best of friends! *I think that's great!* You never know what God will do with the friendship that happens between roommates. Great bands have been started because two roommates started making music together. Huge businesses have begun because a couple of roommates were up at 1 a.m. brain farting together about what the world needs. And even a couple of amazing ministries were started by a couple of good-hearted, big-dreaming roommates. The possibilities are endless. The bond that is possible between roommates can often change your life.

- ○ **PRAY FOR YOUR ROOMMATE.** Even now, before you know him or her, begin asking God to have His hand on your roommate and your relationship. Whether your dormmate is a Christian or not, praying for him or her is important. And it prepares your heart for the challenges that may (or may not) lie ahead.

- ○ **HAVE A SECRET CODE.** Just in case you need a little privacy, come up with a plan (something hung on the doorknob should work) to let your roommate know when entrance into the dorm could mean entering a danger zone. Sometimes, you just need time alone. Of course, you and your roommate share the room and the expenses, so you'll have to be aware that it's not *mandatory* that you or your roommate always obey the code. But, if nothing else, communicating your need to be alone, or get your homework done, or whatever else arises, could encourage your roommate to do her homework elsewhere or, at least, enter with eyes closed.

A FEW MORE POINTERS ABOUT RELATIONSHIPS

CALL HOME ONCE A WEEK – *AT LEAST*. Let Mom and Dad or a guardian know you're okay—or not okay. Gosh, they raised you, so the least you could do is include them in on the fun, excitement, frustrations, and work that come with college life. And yes, talk to your siblings once in a while, too. And Granny, too!

IF YOU MAKE A MISTAKE, MAKE IT RIGHT. You're bound to screw up when it comes to dealing with people, but an apology and the desire to make it right go a long way. Usually, a person will be open to your "I'm sorry," but if they aren't, know that you did the right thing.

MAKE YOURSELF GET INVOLVED IN THOSE CHEESY FRESHMAN ORIENTATION GAMES. It doesn't matter how ridiculous you might feel walking onto a football field with a thousand other students to play some stupid water-balloon game meant to introduce you to people you don't know. Just do it; you're almost guaranteed to be glad you did. And if you don't, e-mail me and I'll apologize.

TALK TO AT LEAST TWO PEOPLE IN EVERY ONE OF YOUR FIRST CLASSES. Be sure to tell them if they look like Matthew Broderick or any other actor for that matter, because people really like that, I hear.

DO NOT START DATING THE FIRST WEEK YOU'RE AT COLLEGE. You know this, right? You weren't even considering it, huh? *Yeah, right.* For those of you who were wondering why I didn't talk about dating, I'll be spending more time on this topic in the next chapter, but I thought this needed to be on the "advice" list for all you people who can't seem to go a month without hooking up. Some of you will be like kids in a candy store your first week at college.

RESIST THE EVANGELICAL URGE TO WITNESS TO ALL OF YOUR NEW FRIENDS THE FIRST WEEK AT SCHOOL. They will probably like you a lot more if you keep the conversation friendly and not fierce. Let God open those doors; you stay away from the doorknob, okay?

《 》

Don't settle for mediocre relationships; instead, pursue the very best that God has for you while at college. Many of the people I met at college are now some of my closest friends, good acquaintances, or even colleagues. You never know why God puts a person in your life. It might be to help you, or you might end up helping him or her. The people skills you practice and learn in college will become either good or bad habits that you practice in life afterward. And how you treat people will tell much more about the real *you* than your grades, your work ethic, or your talent.

FACT: Michael Stipe and Peter Buck of the popular band R.E.M. were once roommates. Obviously, they made it work.

THE CONCLUDING LIST

The five things you must memorize from chapter 2 before moving on!

1. RELATIONSHIPS ARE KEY TO THE COLLEGE EXPERIENCE. Now, say this phrase twenty times, then write it ten times and once backwards. Sure, you can use your journal!

2. YOUR ROOMMATE MIGHT END UP BEING INSANE! It's true; you never know what you'll get out of a roommate, but as you learned earlier, she also might end up *simply* being weird! So you should get down on your knees and pray for your roommate right now. Go ahead and do it. I'll wait right here until you're finished. . . . . Okay already, your prayer doesn't need to be *that* long.

3. KNOW YOUR STRENGTHS. Remember? You wrote them down in your journal earlier! And if you didn't, you are weak, very weak; you should most definitely ignore this line.

4. VISITING A CHURCH MIGHT HELP YOU FIND FRIENDS. And do not feel the least bit funny about having to find a good friend at church. It could be worse; you could be calling 911 just to have someone to talk to. See? Life seems pretty good now, huh?

5. BE YOURSELF! Or at least, a slightly cleaned-up version of yourself! You rock—when you're cleaned up.

COLLEGE IS LIKE A FOUNTAIN
OF KNOWLEDGE – AND THE STUDENTS
ARE THERE TO DRINK.

– AUTHOR UNKNOWN

CHAPTER 3

LIFESTYLE

(Oh boy, now I get to talk about dating, parties, late nights, dorm life, sports, and diversity. This is going to be a good chapter; I can feel it.)

It is not length of life, but depth of life.
— RALPH WALDO EMERSON

WHEN I FIRST WALKED across the campus of Belmont University in Nashville, Tennessee, a big goofy grin covered my face as I looked around at my new home away from home. That smile signaled a very real "college" emotion inside my gut—a mix of excitement, awe, and anticipation for what was to come. As a nineteen-year-old transfer student from a community college in rural Maryland, everything I felt that day was very new to me.

My new surroundings, with all of their mystery, wonder, and grandeur, overwhelmed me a bit. The people I saw gathering in circles with guitars and djembes, tossing footballs and Frisbees, and lying on blankets in the sunshine seemed to bring the campus to life. Sure, the buildings gave Belmont its foundation, but it was the people who made it breathe. Each individual added a certain personality to the campus that would have been absent had they not attended.

Each new encounter or sighting or experience on that first day became more exciting than the last. Whether it was hearing a debate about Jesus between students while they sipped coffee at the rotunda, or sitting inside one of the old campus gazebos and watching for attractive college girls, or buying that first "Belmont" T-shirt, the experiences on that first day at college made me feel alive—more alive than I had ever felt before.

Because I had lived a very sheltered life thus far, I was nothing less than thrilled to finally be in an environment where education, community, growth, and creativity would become my most important and cherished priorities. Of course, some of that "first-day thrill" wore off three days later when I realized how in over my head I was, trying to manage the workload of eighteen credits. But every part of the college experience, even the not-so-good parts, was exciting to me—the learning, the basketball games, the mission trips, the late-night parties, the conversations I had with my best friends until 3 a.m., the make-out sessions with my girlfriend in the gazebos, the classes, the running out of money, and all the stupid things I encountered.

Even today, nearly every time I walk onto a college campus, almost any college campus—no matter its size or beauty or location or historic significance—I still get a taste of that *feeling* I experienced when I walked across Belmont for the very first time. I believe that's true for most former college students. Because most college students go to school with an open mind, a big dream, and a boundless energy for life, the memory of those emotions thickly returns at any campus visit.

Nothing else you experience will be like college—*nothing*. College gives you the chance to meet people from all over the world, and it offers you the opportunity to do things that you might never be able to try again, things like being in a theater production, playing *extremely* competitive sports, or coming into contact with smart *and* attractive people without leaving your dorm room. Or best yet, you might be able to dress up as your school's mascot. WOW! I know you're excited about that. But that's what the lifestyle of college is all about—trying new things and experiencing old things with a fresh perspective.

I know it's your desire to have a college experience that is exciting, adventurous, and over-the-top! Heck, you're probably excited about it being one of the only times in your life when you'll be able to eat pizza at 11:30 at night and not feel the least bit guilty. *Won't that be great!* But this new experience won't be nearly as cool as you think unless you're willing to jump in with complete abandon. In other words, college is only as good as you make it. So you can either walk into this experience with your eyes open and be proactively prepared for what might come your way, or you can be unprepared and let this coming experience swallow you whole. Okay, so it probably won't swallow you whole, but you get what I'm talking about, right?

So get ready; you're about to learn how to make your college lifestyle experience better than you could ever imagine! Or at least, better than it would have been without this book. But since you're reading this book, I guess you'll never know. Hmm.

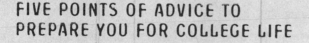

FIVE POINTS OF ADVICE TO PREPARE YOU FOR COLLEGE LIFE

1. HAVE AN OPEN MIND AND HEART. It's easy for us Christians to walk into a new experience and judge every new thing we encounter, or expect to share our faith without expecting to learn from others. Resist the temptation to do this. Having an open mind does not mean you're embracing an idea or person as a belief or a best friend. But it means you're willing to listen and hear someone's story. That's important in college.

2. VALUE WHAT YOU KNOW TO BE TRUE. This is about your faith but also other key areas of your life. Although college might alter the things you hold dear or bring you new insight into those things, knowing and understanding the truth that you bring onto the campus will help keep you grounded. College can be challenging to our values. More than likely, your personal truth might be tested and tempted, but if you believe in something, and more important, if you know *why* you believe in something, you will be better prepared for what you might encounter on your campus.

3. GO TO COLLEGE WITH A "CHANGE THE WORLD" MENTALITY.* To some of you, the idea of changing the world might be overrated or too macro of an idea for you to grasp, but a person with that kind of spirit can be quite influential on a campus. Don't be overwhelmed with how big or small your college might be; go into the experience ready to make a difference. It's that kind of attitude that will help you go places, not only on your campus, but also in your community, city, and world.

4. BE PREPARED TO ENCOUNTER ANYTHING. I know that some of you are pretty naïve about the world. And there's nothing wrong with that. Believe me, I was very inexperienced at life when I attended college, too. But with naivety comes the tendency to judge or become emotionally weighed down by what you encounter. Every college student, no matter what his background, needs to develop some thick skin for what might come – because, I ain't gonna lie, some of you are going to encounter some pretty wild and crazy living while you're at college. And if you do, remember you're not the world's judge. If you're a Christian, you're called to be a light (which most often means "candlelight," since they didn't have spotlights and 1,000-watt bulbs in Jesus' time).

5. ASK GOD TO REVEAL HIS PLAN FOR YOU. Again, communicating with God about the lifestyle of college will allow your mind and heart to be open to what He has for you in this new experience.

---

* It's likely that your dream to "change the world" will change and be tested and bombarded with negativity throughout your life. Don't become discouraged when you feel like you've hit a dead end in your quest to do something big with your life. "Change the world" is a great dream to embrace; it's also a really good song by Eric Clapton.

TEN BIG MISTAKES FRESHMEN OFTEN MAKE THEIR FIRST SEMESTER

1. DATE TOO MUCH TOO FAST TOO SOON. Okay, all together now, *breathe!* You're at college, not on "The Real World." Morality, values, *and* standards are actually all *really* good things! Besides, dating too soon gets in the way of why you're at college—to learn. Remember? You don't need the added stress, time constraint, or emotional weight, at least not for a semester or two.

2. PARTY TOO HARD. Yes, I know that *everyone* around you drinks, but if everyone suddenly decided to pierce their genitalia . . . You get my point? Many times students who party too hard too quickly end up suffering in the classroom, or they get a reputation. Believe me; you don't want that kind of reputation. I have friends who are *still* trying to live down their rep.

3. PROCRASTINATE. Yes, this *is* beginning to sound like a list of the same mistakes you made in high school. But what you don't know is this: College classes are usually much more difficult to keep up with, and you can get far behind *very* quickly! And really, who wants to get left behind?

4. AVOID GETTING INVOLVED. Don't sit on your butt all semester long without getting involved in a few extracurricular activities. (Look for more on this topic in chapter 7.) Whether it's ministry, sports, residence hall, or student government, most colleges have many options for your selection. Do something with your time other than watching daytime TV or playing Pac-Man all day long.

5. EAT LIKE A PIG. Avoid the freshman-fifteen weight gain! Pizza, fast food, and junk food are YOUR ENEMY. Not like Darth Vader is your enemy, but like a black spider in the middle of your bed is your enemy. Meaning, you don't have to be Luke Skywalker to fix the problem. Use common sense when choosing your diet. (More on this topic later, too.)

6. SMOKE POT. Since you love Jesus and all, you probably wouldn't think about taking drugs. Plus, do you remember Nancy Reagan? Yes, I know you were about two years old when she was popular. But she coined the phrase, "Say NO to Drugs!" And no one should disobey Nancy!

7. HAVE SEX. You might be thinking, *This sounds like the Ten Commandments.* Well, you're wrong, Mr. Smarty Pants! Because if it were the Ten Commandments I'd be using words like covet and idol. So there! Anyway, THOU SHALT NOT make the opposite sex your idols and covet their bodies! Do I need to go any further? It doesn't really matter what *you* think, because I'll be talking some about sex later on.

8. BE OVERLY OPINIONATED. I know you think you know it all. But you don't. Trust me. And even if you do know it all, no one wants to hear it! I can *promise* you that. So be careful not to overstate your opinion. Remember, you're trying to make friends, not Darth Vaders. Plus, if you shut up once in a while, you might actually get smarter.

9. DON'T EXERCISE. Yes, many of you are athletes, and that's great. But by the looks of some of you (Oh yeah, I can see you. Spooky, huh?), I can tell that enough of you aren't athletes to warrant this point being in the book!

10. FORGET TO HAVE FUN. Yes, college is about getting an education, but it's also about growing as an individual. (I said this before.) And having fun is a part of that growth! So make sure you're nurturing your soul by getting and out doing things that are meant for your enjoyment.

EMBRACE THE LIFESTYLE WITH EYES WIDE OPEN*
(Because some parts of the college lifestyle can get a little crazy)

- -

INDEPENDENCE
(Because being free is cool and college is often our first taste of freedom)

We Americans like our independence. Many of us go all out on the Fourth of July as a result of our citizenship in a free nation. In celebrating our freedom, we throw parties, wave flags, bake half-naked in the sunshine, shoot off fireworks, and go to parades. But personal independence, *the time in people's lives when they finally realize they have the freedom to choose whatever they want to choose*, is also something we as people celebrate. And I don't think there's a college student alive who doesn't like his or her independence. For most, it's perhaps the most celebrated and enjoyed part about going to college.

We experience that love for all things "independent" in pop culture. Kelly Clarkson and Destiny's Child sang about it in their songs "Miss Independence" and "Independent Women." Hollywood captured its intensity on screen in the far-fetched alien-invasion movie *Independence Day*. Music lovers often find "independent" music to be more real and less processed than music created on a major label. Those kids in *American Pie* learned a thing or two about the "free life" when they attempted to take full advantage of their sexual freedoms. And a quick "independent" search at Amazon.com garners thousands of titles ranging from a historical novel about America's Revolutionary War to one that emphasizes the importance of being independent in relationships to one about finding freedom to be "yourself" in the workplace.

College is that time in life when many young adults (certainly not all) get to experience their own independence. And I'm sure

---

* Did anyone other than me think of that really annoying song by Creed when reading this title? Yes, I know it's "With *Arms* Wide Open." But it's close. Do you now have the tune stuck in your head? Good. I hope it stays there all day long.

the thought of being free, *really* free, from parental control has you singing your own slightly altered version of "The Star-Spangled Banner." For most guys, knowing they'll never again have to listen to Mom demand that they pick up their room is almost as sweet as the thought of Angelina Jolie in *Tomb Raider*. I said *almost*. And girls, you have to admit that some kind of unexplainable and wonderful feeling happens inside of your gut when you think about *never* having to ask your father if you're allowed to stay out until 11 p.m. *(GASP!)*

You're not alone in your feelings. Even the most conservative of future freshmen is looking forward to not feeling *burdened* to follow a few of his parents' rules. And all of those feelings are completely natural when you're getting ready to leave for college. Let's face it; there's just something incredibly exciting about finally being able to make a decision without your parents being around. *WOW*.

Okay, so some of you are rolling your eyes right now because you're thinking, "I don't know what you're talking about; I make my own decisions." And I have no doubt that you're right about that. I'm sure you've encountered many situations throughout your teenage years where you have had the freedom to make up your own mind. But since most of you, up until this moment, have been under the watchful eyes of your mom and dad or another legal guardian, you were no doubt influenced by their leadership. And that's a good thing.

But since you're going to college, that's about to change quite a bit. When you're at college, your newfound independence can either push you to grow (spiritually, mentally, emotionally), or it can limit you in all of those same areas.

Hate to break it to you, but with all of that new college freedom you've won, you also get a rather lame parting gift — a lot more responsibility.

FOUR VERSES FROM PSALM 16 THAT EVERY COLLEGE STUDENT SHOULD KNOW

Day and night I'll stick with God;
> I've got a good thing going and I'm not letting go.

I'm happy from the inside out,
> and from the outside in, I'm firmly formed.
You canceled my ticket to hell –
> that's not my destination!

Now you've got my feet on the life path,
> all radiant from the shining of your face.
Ever since you took my hand,
> I'm on the right way. (verses 8-11)

Simon Diggs* is a sophomore at a medium-sized school in Arizona. When he left for college last year, he considered himself to be a pretty good kid. However, his parents believed he was the *best* of kids. Sending him to a large state school with 17,000 students didn't worry them at all. They had seen him make good choices throughout his high-school experience, so they believed he would do nothing but the same while at college.

"My parents kept me sheltered," wrote Simon via e-mail. "I made 'good' decisions before college because I didn't have a choice; my parents watched me like I was a ticking time bomb. And honestly, I

---

* Name is changed.

didn't mind it. In fact, I never thought too much about the rules."

During the first two months of Simon's freshman year, he said the word "no" a lot. When he was asked to join a buddy of his at a party, he refused. When a girl he was kind of dating asked him to stay overnight in her dorm, he made up an excuse not to. When he caught his room-mate looking at porn on the computer, he admits to being curious, but he ended up just leaving the room.

"That was a hard couple of months," he admitted. "I was begin-ning to realize that I was not making these choices out of my personal convictions; I was making these decisions because I feared that some-how my mom and dad would find out what I had done. I learned quickly that 'fearing your parents catching word about your life' won't keep you out of trouble."

Eventually, Simon grew tired of saying no. Because of a little consis-tent coaxing from a couple of his college friends, Simon decided to go with them to a party at one of the college frat houses. Before that night, he had tasted beer only twice in his life. However, during that particular party, Simon found out that his tall, 235-pound frame gave him a pretty high alcohol tolerance. So, in an effort to secure a good buzz, Simon kept drinking until he was one of the drunkest at the party.

That night became the first of many parties that Simon attended during his freshman year. By the time he left school to go home for the summer vacation, Simon had experienced a lot of firsts that weren't quite as healthy as, say, his first time to Disneyland. According to Simon, his new freedom brought him a lot of popularity, "luck with the ladies," and a newfound respect among his friends. At the time that Simon agreed to do this interview, his parents were still unaware of their son's new life. Simon planned to do his best to keep it that way.*

For many, the independence of college overwhelms and chal-lenges, but for others, the freedom that comes with the college life

---

* When Simon began his sophomore year at college, he contacted one of the Fellowship of Christian Athletes (FCA) leaders on campus. Through accountability and connection with his FCA group, Simon's making a second go at independence.

creates opportunity to be influential, successful, and creative. Consider twenty-six-year-old Janel Whitley's answer to this question:

WHAT DOES COLLEGE INDEPENDENCE MEAN TO YOU?

As a Christian, I believe the freedom we experience while at college should push us to be more successful. When I went to college, my sister gave me this good advice: "Being independent is not about you getting what you want, Janel; it's about being free to serve the people and the community around you." I took those words to heart. So during that first week of college, instead of seeking out friends who knew where the closest and wildest parties were, I sought out opportunities to get involved in college life. With only a little effort, I found information about ministries, college associations, and local charities where I could invest my time. Too many people associate freedom with going out and "breaking the rules." But I believe if you really begin to see freedom as a call to serve instead of be served, your college life will be enhanced through those experiences.

THOUGHTS (FROM OTHER PEOPLE) ABOUT INDEPENDENCE

True independence and freedom can only exist in doing what's right.
> —BRIGHAM YOUNG, a well-known Mormon leader

Mickey Mouse is, to me, a symbol of independence. He was a means to an end.
> —WALT DISNEY, the man behind the magic of everything Disney

Independence is happiness.
> —SUSAN B. ANTHONY
> (I once carried a "Susan B. Anthony" around in my pocket)

BUSYNESS

(Because at least three times during your college career, you're going to think to yourself, Is this really worth it?*)*

Possibly the most overwhelming college lifestyle component, other than having to stand in line at your school's bookstore, is *busyness*. Just plan on this: You will be busy. Once students get in the college grind, many of them realize quickly that the schedule they kept in high school was cake compared to the busyness of college. From getting up in the early morning for classes to fitting in some kind of weekly exercise to working fifteen hours a week at a part-time job to squeezing in a few extra-curricular activities, the average college lifestyle is fast-paced, mind-boggling, and prone to making you feel like a stressed-out mess.

But fear not, for behold, I bring you great advice for staying sane.

[1] Do not add more to your plate than you can handle. [2] Do you not know how added stress can only bring you down? [3] Why do you worry so much about going here and going there? [4] While in your haste you forget about the things that truly matter. [5] Do you not know that it's important to plan out your life like it's a road map? You will accomplish more if you know what needs to be accomplished. [6] Didn't the Prophet Mom warn you about your inability to handle so much? Didn't she say, "Let go of what's silly and take hold of only the things that truly matter"? [7] So know this to be true: Passionately take hold of what's educational, communal, and spiritual, for it's in these things that true success is found.

A STUDY GUIDE TO PREVIOUS TEXT

1. It's simple to just keep saying yes when you're asked to volunteer or to join a club or another study group, but here is some advice on knowing how much you actually can handle. Some of you can handle a great

deal—you're masters at organizing—but others of you are more apt to become overwhelmed by a heavy workload.

2. These words are self-explanatory. If you become stressed, your ability to finish even the simplest of projects will be more difficult. Stress, if not managed, can bring down even the best college student.

3. Think about your daily routine. Ask yourself this question: Are there priorities in your life that you deem important that might not be necessary to your college lifestyle? I'm not saying that you should avoid fun, but I am suggesting that some of the things you create time for might be hurting rather than helping your journey toward success.

4. If your workload at college becomes overwhelming, it's easy to lose focus. So this piece of advice suggests that you should plan now to make good decisions about your schedule so you can avoid being consumed by the busyness.

5. Once in a while, no matter how much you do to avoid feeling stressed, all of the important parts of life will have a deadline on the same day. You should plan ahead, keeping track of all that you need to get completed so you will be able to finish your tasks and avoid procrastinating.

6. This simply suggests that you should listen to the advice of others, especially your mom, dad, and other mentors. They will help keep you from overloading your life with unnecessary tasks.

7. Simply put, I believe that while at college, the things that truly matter are school, your friends, and your faith. In the midst of your busyness, make these three your priorities.

PRACTICAL ADVICE ABOUT BUSYNESS

As you plan and schedule all that you need to get finished in a semester, be sure to organize personal "alone" time into your calendar. With all that happens during college life, taking time to be alone once in a while will help you organize your thoughts. And you *could* pick up that journal and write down your thoughts, but I won't push that at the moment. Even if your alone time is spent shopping or hiking or sitting at Starbucks reading a novel, time by yourself gives you a chance to refuel. With all the busyness, you'll need to refuel.

DATING
(Because you might just meet someone you believe is worth spending a lot of time with)

Okay, so here's the deal: Dating at college is a good thing. In fact, I'll even go so far as to say that I personally recommend it. Think about this: College might be the only time in your life where you'll be surrounded by thousands of smart, available people just waiting to be snatched up in the trap of *love*.

However, dating should not be your focus while in college. Though some certainly find their lifetime mate while studying to be an engineer or doctor, if you go to college with the mind-set that you're there only to get hitched, you're seriously limiting your personal potential. Then again, those who go to college thinking, *I am not going to even think about dating*, might very well be limiting their potential, too. You have no clue what God has in store for your life, so keep your mind and heart open to His possibilities, and not your own.

With all of that said, I mention dating in this book because frankly *dating* seems to happen when boys and girls are in close proximity to each other. And it can be a very good thing. In fact, I believe, if pursued in the right way, dating can actually be an integral part of the college lifestyle. Unfortunately, many students are quick to make it the *most important* part of their college experience. Some college students jump in and out of relationships as often as Oprah's mug lands on the cover of her own magazine. (That's every month, for those of you who live unusually sheltered lives.) But who am I kidding? I can't possibly cover everything about dating and college in one section of one book. Moreover, many books exist that talk about Christians and dating (although most of them make me sick to my stomach). I'll recommend a few later. So I'm simply going to list the pros and cons of dating at college here and let you decide (you're an adult now, right?) how you should proceed.

THE BATMAN AND JOKER OF DATING AT COLLEGE

(In other words, the good *and* bad *of seeing someone when you're supposed to be getting an education)*

GOOD: Options. You will more than likely meet many fascinating, well-adjusted, and attractive individuals while in college. Believe me, good guys and girls are hard to find.

BAD: Unfocused. Dating can cause even the most organized and smart college student to become seriously ADHD. Think Phoebe on *Friends*. She's a ditz, right? Despite how healthy a relationship might be, the amount of attention you have to give it can cause an earthquake in the brain *and heart*.

GOOD: Easy. It's easy to date at college. Being at the same college makes time and dates and getting to know the *real* him or her simpler.

BAD: Easy. All of what I just mentioned in that last "good" point can also lead to a relationship becoming boring, unhealthy, or downright psychotic.

GOOD: Accountability. Okay, so I am not a fan of this word. But sadly, it's the only word that seems to make sense. If you and your significant other are smart, you will seek out friends and mentors to help you keep the relationship healthy. College provides easy access to that.

BAD: Sex. Since you're probably not planning on getting married until you're out of college, the physical aspect of a relationship is an important facet to consider when thinking about dating. Believe me, I know so many college students who have said, "Oh, that will never be a problem for me." But when you're young, turned on, and alone in a comfortable place, "stuff" can get out of hand. (I'll talk more about sex soon.)

Of course, I'm sure there are countless good and bad reasons to date at college—certainly too many to count here. But like much of the college experience, dating truly depends on the individual. When dating, the best thing to remember is this: A relationship with someone should push you to be your best in every area of your life—school, faith, relationships, and so on. And remember that you should be doing the same for your significant other. If that's not happening, it's probably best to not date that person. Too often, but not always, eighteen- to twenty-one-year-olds aren't emotionally prepared to make the kind of commitment needed to keep a college relationship healthy. And not being ready for *that kind of* commitment is okay as long as you're *not* dating someone. If you know you're not ready, then help yourself and don't date.

BOOKS ON BEING CHRISTIAN AND DATING

- *Boundaries in Dating* by Dr. Henry Cloud and Dr. John Townsend
- *Choices: Finding God's Way in Dating, Sex, Singleness, and Marriage* by Stacy Rinehart and Paula Rinehart
- *5 Paths to the Love of Your Life* by Lauren F. Winner, et al.

THREE DOS OF DATING
(Because you need to consider a lot before dating)

1. DO WAIT A SEMESTER. School is hard enough without having to invest time into a "committed" relationship. If the attraction is there in October of your freshman year, it will likely be there in February of your freshman year and might even be there when you're a sophomore. So breathe and don't rush into something that's going to potentially make life more stressful for you.

2. DO BECOME FRIENDS, FIRST AND FOREMOST. This is hard, I know, but building a friendship before you begin dating is *always* good. It's through friendship that we truly get to know a person's character. If you can at all avoid getting into a bad relationship during college, it will save you from a lot of pain, frustration, and wasted time.

3. DO KNOW YOU. Just as I mentioned in the last chapter about the importance of knowing *you* when pursuing friendships, you need to know what you bring to the table before you begin dating, too. If it's neediness and the tendency to become codependent, or if it's merely a sex drive like Colin Farrell's, then avoid dating during college. You'll only make more problems for yourself if you date.

A "BEFORE YOU DATE" BONUS

DO AVOID BECOMING IN ANY WAY PHYSICAL WITH SOMEONE WITHOUT HAVING A "DEFINE THE RELATIONSHIP" TALK (DTR) FIRST. Even if you know there's an attraction, talk about it *before* you begin holding hands, kissing, and the like. Often, when you're in the heat of the moment, you think more with your genitalia than with your head and heart – and you'd be surprised at how often you feel differently after you have slept it off.

SEX
(Because even at the most conservative colleges it's easy to mess up)

Despite being pretty darn sure that you already know this, I feel compelled to repeat it just so you can hear it again for the millionth time: God has designed sex to be within the bond of marriage. But you knew that, right? Yeah, I thought so. Believe me, I once foolishly wished I could find a "biblical" way around this one, but it's *not* there. I've looked. And now that I am married, I understand why God created sex to be experienced *only* within marriage. But that's hard to explain to someone who is eighteen and in college. And it's even harder to live it when you're eighteen and in college.

But trust me, before I became *spiritually* informed on the godly principles of sex, college life certainly tested my personal desire to remain *untouched* until marriage. Nearly every person I spoke to about their college experience found that the fight to uphold the life-of-celibacy-until-marriage thing that Christians desire was quite difficult during their college years. Here are a few of the comments I received:

My wife and I started dating our junior year in college, and we made an agreement that we wouldn't go beyond kissing. Although we slipped a little past kissing a couple of times, we remained pure by opening up to our friends and our young adult pastor about our struggle. It was in those relationships, and also in spending time with God together, that we were able to wait until our wedding night — and then we went all out.

— PATRICK, 27, ALUM OF UNIVERSITY OF TEXAS

Despite knowing what the Bible taught about sex, an unhealthy desire to feel loved and accepted brought me a wealth of trouble in my relationships. Sadly, I didn't wait for sex until marriage. In my one serious relationship with a Christian guy, I had sex with him just so he wouldn't break up with me. Yes, I was that insecure. Two weeks after we had sex, he couldn't handle the guilt. So he broke up with me. I wish I could go back.

— DANIELLE, 25, ALUM OF TULANE UNIVERSITY

During college I fell into the "friends with benefits" lie. I had numerous random hookups. Surprisingly, I didn't have sex; I just did everything but. . . . In the process, I hurt a lot of girls. My reputation was pretty much trashed by the time I graduated.

— TED, 23, ALUM OF LIBERTY UNIVERSITY

I didn't have a problem with sex in college. But that might be because I never dated.

— HOPE, 22, ALUM OF FLORIDA STATE

The whole purity versus lust battle is difficult *throughout* one's post-pubescent life. But often, it's those final years of high school and the beginning years at college where the battle gets extremely difficult. For most of the Christians I talked to, it was during college that the real war began. Most of those people cited youth groups, parents, and undefined faith as reasons why remaining pure wasn't nearly as difficult in high school. James, a twenty-nine-year-old graduate of Bethel College, had this to say about sex and college: "My parents didn't let me date in high school. So when I went to college, I made up for lost time. I made dating my lifestyle. And I ended up screwing around *a lot* in college."

While at college, probably almost *any* college, it's quite possible that sex or sexual activity will be a temptation. However, each individual is different. Each school is different. Each situation is very different. Good advice for one student is nothing more than ridiculous jargon to another. Not shocking, I had more than a couple people tell me that sex was never a temptation for them. And it might not be for you. But do you know where you stand on the issue? Do you know what you believe is too far? What if you end up putting yourself in a situation you never dreamed would be possible?

Eva Marie Everson, along with her daughter Jessica, talk about sex all of the time—in front of churches, colleges, and cameras. In some strange way, I suppose they're Christian *sexperts*. But the one thing that struck me about the Eversons is the amount of research they include in their advice.

After meeting them at a women's conference where we were both speaking, I thought Eva might have some insight she could offer for this book. I have to tell you, though, her answers are frank and honest. At first, they might seem a little dogmatic to some of you (at first, they were to me, too). But having met Eva, I know she is a person with a heart to help people resist the temptation of sex before marriage. Even if you disagree with a few of Eva's opinions, I believe her answers will help you make good, well-informed choices when it comes to sex.

MATTHEW: In your opinion, what are the scariest statistics involving sex and college students?

EVA: Honestly, a lot scares me. I hear so many awful stories about Christian young men and porn. The same is true for Christian unmarried couples engaging in sexual activity. Some of the stories I hear are overwhelming.

In my research, I have found that so many college girls have set up web cams for quick money and are literally prostituting themselves for the point of a dollar. They aren't having sex with the one paying, so they don't see it as prostituting. But, I believe it is. They are selling more than their bodies; they are selling a part of their souls.

The other information that is upsetting is about STDs. Years ago a girl worried about getting pregnant. But today, a pregnancy can be dealt with. It's not necessarily an easy choice, but there are adoptions, raising the child with the help of family and friends, raising the child alone, marriage, and sadly, abortion. STDs are another animal altogether. They have lingering, life-altering effects. These can be passed down to children.

What most people don't know is that our country has one of the highest STD rates in the world. The majority of those infected are within the young-adult bracket (under twenty-five). Sadly, the damage that can be done is never truly considered when one is in the throes of passion.

MATTHEW: Why do you think that most students in today's culture don't view oral sex as sex?

EVA: Thank you, Mr. President [Clinton]. Please don't take this as a political statement. It's not. This is a moral statement. Today's students think that anything outside penile/vaginal sex is not sex. But the Bible teaches differently. When God speaks of sexual immorality, He doesn't just speak of traditional sex. I believe He pretty much talked the whole talk there. It's important to understand that purity is not simply walking the "virginity" line; it's about being entirely pure—our hearts, minds, and bodies. The Bible says we're to be living sacrifices, and anything involving lust is not, in my opinion, being a living sacrifice.

MATTHEW: Do you have any wisdom for college couples who desire a pure relationship?

EVA: Look, I wasn't pure as a teen. I was pregnant at sixteen. But, after I prayed to God for help (and then lost the baby), I stayed pure until I married my husband. It wasn't always easy. In fact, it was quite difficult, and I nearly failed several times. But every time I would remember what happened before. Not the pregnancy, but the feelings of being a little more separated from God . . . the very One I wanted to draw closest to. The very One I wanted to please the most. And I'd ask myself, "Is this worth it? Is this worth hurting God?"

Some sins won't change your life forever. And sex outside of marriage is indeed sin. Media can't wish that away or change God's mind. Too many young people aren't going to the Bible for the answers or for guidance or instruction.

Sure, some sins won't change your life forever, but sex will alter your life. It will change how you feel about yourself . . . and about the one you are with. It will turn friends into strangers. It will change how others feel about you. It can bring another life into the world . . . an innocent little life . . . or it can take yours out. But most important, it will cause separation between you and God. But I believe the Bible teaches that God cannot be in the presence of non-holiness. Strangely, whenever the Bible talks about being holy . . . somehow that "sexual immorality" term keeps coming up.

MATTHEW: In your opinion, is there a line that is too far?

EVA: Yes, absolutely. A young friend of mine is a musician and very passionate about everything he does. He has been "in love" for two years now. Knowing himself well, he has decided not to kiss this young woman until they say, "I do." But I know others who say kissing is fine, but that's it. Anything else and most people are going to be dealing with a decision to make and a physical struggle against spiritual truth.

FACTS: Stats about sex and college students are often misleading.

- A study by the University of North Carolina states that one in two sexually active college-age students will contract a sexually transmitted disease by age twenty-five.[1]
- Fifty-six percent of college students who live far from home are having sex. Seventy-three percent of those are having unprotected sex.[2]
- According to a 2005 unscientific online study, two-thirds (66 percent) of women (ages 18–24) surveyed reported that they are in committed relationships while only one-third (38 percent) of men (ages 18–24) reported the same.
- In this study, 18 percent of the women reported being virgins, compared with 34 percent of men.

CLEARING UP MISCONCEPTIONS ABOUT SEX
(Just in case you did not know)

- Oral sex is indeed sex. It doesn't take your "technical virginity" away, but it is sex, nonetheless.
- Mutual masturbation is sex, too. Just thought I would go ahead and throw that out there.
- You can get STDs from both of the above practices. Condoms should be used. *I am not condoning sex by suggesting the use of a condom, but if you're going to sin, do it at least 98.3 percent safer.* Most studies suggest that Christians will engage in unprotected sex more often than non-Christians.
- If you feel you have a problem with sex, get help. I know it might seem embarrassing to talk about your desires with a professional, but it will help you create healthy (and godly) thinking about sex.
- Remaining pure until marriage is not only God's design; it's also the safest. But I'm not going to lie; that can be very difficult to do

sometimes when you're in college. That's why it's important to be communicating with someone other than your roommate or best friend or Bible study leader—talk to a professional.

DORM LIFE
(Because you'll be spending an awful lot of time there)

Dorm life is much more than simply a place to sleep and keep all of your belongings. Yes, your room is merely a large box with a couple of beds that you have to *share* with one or two other residents, but the dorm will also be the place where you find a great deal of your college community. Many of your strongest and most cherished relationships will begin in this upcoming first year in the dorm. (You may eventually move out of the boxy-styled dorms and opt for a plush apartment-styled dorm, or you'll move off campus with a couple of your dearest friends.) However, while you're living in the dorms, take full advantage of experiencing the dorm life to capacity.

So if you're a bit fearful of the dorm life or if you simply want a few ideas to enhance your experience, the following list of ideas (some practical, some creative, and some just downright necessary) will help you adjust to your brand-new, even if it is a little old and smelly, living arrangement.

A FEW WAYS TO MAKE DORM LIFE BETTER

1. GET TO KNOW YOUR RESIDENT ASSISTANT (RA). Build a good relationship with "the trained professional" down the hall (he or she is usually one of the best and brightest juniors and/or seniors the college has to offer—though sometimes that isn't saying much). Getting to know him or her might make dorm life a little easier for you.

2. OBEY EVEN THE "STUPID" RULES. Every college has a few seemingly pointless rules for dorm life. They range from enforced quiet hours after 10 p.m. to no George Foreman grills permitted inside the dorms to no televisions allowed in the rooms. Yes, to some, a few of the rules are silly. But no matter how much you *love* the smell of vanilla-scented candles burning while you study or how much you need a microwave oven so you can make popcorn, obeying the rules makes dorm life, according to the university, safer for all.

3. DECORATE YOUR ROOM LIKE IT'S YOUR OWN. Mark your territory with a little style. Of course, this doesn't mean, ladies, that you should dress it up in all things Pottery Barn or, guys, pee in the corners. But dorm life is always better when you've thrown a little bit of yourself—your creative personality, family history (pictures), design expertise, and the bedspread of your choice—around the room.

4. WEAR FLIP-FLOPS IN THE SHOWER. Things get left in the shower. And I'm not talking about small bottles of shampoo and conditioner. If you don't wear some kind of footwear when you're naked and attempting to get clean, you have a good chance of coming into contact with something icky—for instance, E. coli, athlete's foot, meningitis, or somebody else's pubic hair. And really, the thought of somebody else's pubic hair touching the bottom of your foot should make you want to wear protection.

5. BE INVOLVED IN DORM ACTIVITIES. Whether these activities involve pizza, board games, studying, a Bible and group of friends, or all of the above, dorm activities (especially during the first couple weeks of school) are probably the best ways to build relationships with others.

6. HANG OUT IN THE COMMON AREA WITH FRIENDS AND THE TV. Whether it's for watching sporting events, *The Bachelor*, *Lost*, or *Seinfeld* reruns, gathering around the TV (usually located in the common area of most dorm floors) is a way to hang out with those you love and those you don't yet know. Even with the TV on, this provides a great opportunity to get to know the people who live in the dorm with you. (BTW: Even if you hate the shows your dormmates watch, hang out just for the friendliness of it all!)

7. START A DORM SMALL GROUP OR BIBLE STUDY. For some of you, this might be borderline cheesy, and that's okay—to each his own. But for others of you, beginning a small group with some friends is a great way to remain spiritually focused during college. Make your small group open to all or simply a group of your closest friends. Don't complicate it. Just have fun with it.

8. ADD A BIT OF YOUR PERSONALITY TO YOUR DOOR. Put pictures up on your door, decorate it for the holidays, or even hang a dry erase board on it and write up a few random quotes. Just let people know your (wild or quiet or thoughtful) personality by displaying it on your door.

DIVERSITY

(Because we're all different in one way or another)

One of the best parts of the college experience is having the opportunity to meet and interact with a wide variety of people. Of course, the spectrum of diversity greatly depends on the college you attend. Certain colleges are known to be well-established breeding grounds for extensive ranges of diversity. Colleges like UCLA, American University, University of Miami, and NYU are just a few schools among the many known for attracting people from different countries, cultures, and religions. Today, many colleges put an enormous amount of time, budget, and effort into creating a welcoming campus environment for students of diversity. And that's a great thing, because you will get to see and experience life from many different vantage points.

However, differences in cultures and religions are simply the beginning of the kinds of diversity you might encounter while at college. Campuses all over the world are diverse because of ideas and lifestyles, prejudices, and points of view. Even more conservative colleges with Christian roots or Southern geography are today much more open-minded to people from a variety of backgrounds, creeds, and perspectives.

As a college freshman, you should be prepared for almost

anything — and I do mean *anything*. During these upcoming years at college, some of you will encounter an array of thoughts, including ideas about science and God, every kind of sexual orientation, all types of spiritualities and cults, many more political views than just two, and cultural perspectives you've never stumbled upon before. In other words, college is going to give some of you a very real education in the ways of this world we live in. So be willing to learn from what you encounter.

For some, this experience can be overwhelming at first. There's a pretty good chance that the diversity part of your "education" will challenge your own view, perspective, or belief. Being challenged or pushed out of your comfort zone isn't all that enjoyable at times. But it's bound to happen, even if it's not in college; it will no doubt happen at some point in your professional or personal life. Unfortunately, when you're first entering college, you're not always prepared for the different views and ideas of people.

As a person of faith, the most important fundamental truth to understand about diversity is this: It's a Christian's calling to love one's neighbor. Most believe, as do I, that "neighbor" includes all people. It's not simply Jesus followers who are our neighbors. Our "neighbor" is everyone, no matter his creed, ideals, religion, or lifestyle. We as followers of Christ are called to live a lifestyle of truth, love, peace, humility, and grace. At the core of that lifestyle is Jesus' desire for us to love God and love others. "Others" is a broad term here. In fact, "others" covers a diverse array of people. I believe that "others" includes, but is not limited to, frequent drug users, Muslims, jocks who drink too much, Christian fundamentalists, sex addicts, people from China, atheists, Republicans, partiers, the LGBT club at your college, Communists, and those impaired by physical and mental handicaps.

Above all, your most important calling while at college is to build relationships with your neighbors and love them. If it's difficult for you at first, which it is for many college freshmen, don't be okay with it being "hard." Work through the challenges that diversity makes you feel. People tend to resist the stuff that is hard. Instead, pursue learning how to love people who have different views from you. Rest assured that you (and they) will be bettered for the experience.

SEVERAL THINGS YOU DON'T DO WHEN YOU MEET PEOPLE WHO ARE DIFFERENT FROM YOU

- **DON'T HATE.** Why waste one ounce of time and energy on something that accomplishes nothing?
- **DON'T BELIEVE THAT TRUTH ABSENT OF LOVE IS TRUTH.** Just always remember this: The truth of Jesus and the love of Jesus are inseparable.
- **DON'T AVOID ASKING QUESTIONS.** Questions are a good thing. A person who is an atheist likes talking about himself just as much as you do. (But when you're talking, follow the first two rules.)
- **DON'T AVOID BEING A FRIEND.** I have learned something new about Jesus through every relationship with someone who believes differently than I do. In many cases, Jesus speaks to me through the people in my life who I struggle to love more often than through the people who are Christians. *Go figure.*
- **DON'T SAY ANYTHING AT ALL IF YOU CAN'T SAY SOMETHING GOOD.** This needs no punchy sentence.

The lifestyle of college is exciting, but it can certainly offer its share of huge challenges. You'll understand this truth the first time someone asks you to streak across campus in nothing but socks and a pair of shoes. Would *you* do it? That's pretty tempting, huh? You know you'd want to a little bit. Some of you are freaks and you know it. Okay, so maybe that "streaking across campus" scenario really isn't all that challenging, but you'll learn the "challenges" of college one way or another.

However, despite all of the challenges you might experience, college offers opportunities in life that for many come around only once in a lifetime. So make sure you take advantage of every part of the lifestyle that you can—well, at least the ethical, moral, and legal parts of it anyway.

I am concluding this chapter with a list of things you *have got* (yes, I know "have got" is poor English) to do in order to have the best college lifestyle possible.

A PRACTICAL COLLEGE LIFESTYLE CHECKLIST: TWELVE THINGS YOU SHOULD KNOW, LEARN, OR LOCATE BEFORE YOU GET THERE OR WHEN YOU ARRIVE

- -

1. LEARN EVERYTHING YOU CAN ABOUT YOUR COLLEGE CAMPUS. Learn about its history, its trees, and its buildings. Know the main locations. Know where your classes will be held. Find out where the fun is to be had. You should be able to find this information online.

2. LEARN ABOUT THE CITY OR TOWN THAT SURROUNDS YOUR COLLEGE. Learn more about the town than simply where the closest movie theater and Starbucks are located. Find out where you can see concerts, sporting events, shows, and museums. But also, know a little about the town's history. You might consider purchasing a map of the town or city, too.

3. LOCATE YOUR CAMPUS'S MINISTRY OFFICES. Know where you can find spiritual help, if necessary. Introduce yourself to the person in charge.

4. FIND OUT IF YOUR COLLEGE OFFERS FREE COUNSELING. You never know when you might simply need to talk to a trained counselor about life, school, or a relationship.

5. JOURNAL ABOUT YOUR COLLEGE EXPERIENCE. Yes, I know I sound like a broken record, but they say that the average person needs to hear something seven times before he or she will act on it. Dang, I've lost count.

6. LOCATE YOUR COLLEGE'S NURSE, DOCTOR, OR MED UNIT. Whether you're sick or need to speak to someone about everything from medication to sexually transmitted diseases, this office can help.

7. LOCATE ALL OF YOUR CAMPUS'S EMERGENCY CALL BUTTONS. Most colleges have kiosks throughout the campus where you can call for help if needed. Know the locations of these places.

8. LEARN THE *BAD SIDE* OF CAMPUS, TOWN, OR THE CITY. You don't necessarily have to go there, but know where it is so you can avoid being alone in a place that is unsafe. If you are concerned about this, talk to your campus life office. (I'll talk more about safety and security in chapter 5.)

9. KNOW THE NUMBER, JUST IN CASE. This might not be popular for some of you, but I believe it's important that you carry with you the phone number for a safe local cab service in case you ever make a mistake and drink too much at a party. I do not approve of underage drinking, but I do approve of playing it safe.

10. LEARN YOUR COLLEGE'S RESOURCES. If you don't know what your college offers in the way of lifestyle, you can't use it. Talk to your RA or campus life office about all of the little *extras* that might be important for you to know.

11. LEARN ABOUT THE CULTURE OF YOUR CAMPUS. Find out if your college is a huge party school, if it has a particular political or social slant, or if it is a strict, boring school with no life at all. You're going to want to know what to expect when you arrive. You don't want to be *completely* shocked. Give yourself a chance to prepare for what's to come. You'll thank me (or you'll forget that I gave you that tidbit of wisdom and never thank me at all — and I'm okay with that).

THE CONCLUDING LIST

The five things from chapter 3 that you must have written on your back at all times!

1. DIVERSITY IS COOL. While you're at college, make sure you meet people from different cultures, religions, and races. Don't take college diversity for granted; it's a classroom in and of itself.

2. ORAL SEX IS _____(FILL IN THE BLANK). You can do this! It's a three-letter word and ends with the letter x. I sometimes feel sorry for the letter x; if I were it, I would protest and demand to be used more often.

3. FLIP-FLOPS ARE YOUR FRIENDS. They keep your toes from touching gross things.

4. USE SOUND JUDGMENT WHEN EXPLORING YOUR INDEPENDENCE. Just because no one is around to tell you what to do doesn't mean this college thing is a free ticket to do whatever you want. So be wise!

5. LOVE YOUR SCHOOL. Enjoy this time in your life; it happens only once.

INTELLIGENCE PLUS CHARACTER —
THAT IS THE GOAL OF TRUE EDUCATION.

— MARTIN LUTHER KING JR.

CHAPTER 4

EDUCATION

(Because if I'm not mistaken on this, classes, homework, professors, and deadlines are what college is all about)

Without education we are in a horrible and deadly danger of taking educated people seriously.
— G. K. CHESTERTON

I'VE TALKED ABOUT A lot thus far. We've journeyed together through leaving, relating, and living. But I guess any book about college must cover the education part of this future experience. I mean, getting an education *is* the reason you're going to college, right? Of course it is. At least, most of you are going to college for an education. Although, this is not true for all of you. Some of you are going to college because you're being forced to go. Some of you are going in hopes of scoring a college hookup. (You didn't learn much about those odds in high school, huh?) Some of you are going to college because you're good at basketball, track and field, football, or another scholarship-honored competitive sport. And I'm sure a few of you have reasons that I wouldn't be able to repeat.

However, the *majority* of you have your eyes targeted on the prize of the much-coveted college diploma. You're going to college with high hopes of becoming educated on a particular subject or to learn a trade or skill that you plan to use for the rest of your life or to perfect something you're naturally talented at. You're going to college to become mentally or skillfully bettered. College is about getting an education, even if you are one of those students looking for a sexy young coed to marry. Everyone who attends still must suffer through the classes, professors, homework, research papers, and test taking.

For some of you, the education you're planning on receiving (or you're trying to receive) will likely be the grueling, humbling, challenging, send-your-head-into-an-emotional-funk part of your time at college. And learning can certainly make you feel that way once in a while—well, unless you're a modern-day Albert Einstein.

You're not alone when these kinds of feelings arise. The education part of college is difficult for most. Of course, the difficulties one experiences at college greatly depend on the subject he studies and the college he attends. But don't worry, I'm going to help you through the grind of getting an education.

PRACTICAL ADVICE ABOUT EDUCATION

Be sure to see these upcoming four years at college as a jumping-off point for your education. In other words, your education continues way beyond college. If you walk into college with this truth, you're more likely to graduate still desiring to learn from life.

I believe each of you, no matter your major, school, or intelligence level, can find success at college. Success is why you're reading this book, correct? That, and the fact your father or mother just handed it to you and said, "Read this book." You probably looked at him or her and said, "Why should I?" And then, your parent looked at you and said, "Because I got it on sale at Wal-Mart, and I believe it will really help you get prepared for college." I'm *not* offended by your initial reaction to my book. I admit, I've written a somewhat geeky book. I *completely* understand your skepticism. But don't be offended if I take a moment and call my therapist.

Okay, back to the topic of success. I'm quite sure that most of you are hoping the education you receive at college will be a BIG part of what sustains you financially, creatively, and professionally for the rest of your lives. And it's certainly been known to do that from time to time.

However, I want you to know something; success in education can be measured in a lot of different ways—grades, knowledge gained, your personal improvement, participation, and writing skill. Some of you are going to naturally be a little better in certain areas than others. Believe me; that's okay. Fight back the urge to simply look at the grade on your test or report card to measure your success. For some of you, getting a good grade in Statistics 101 is just as easy as failing. For others, you will struggle to get a B- in a stats class. Success is different for each individual; it's personal to your learning styles. Sure, the professor might grade you with the same scale, but how *you* perceive things should be different. Only you know what you're capable of doing. Success is more than just grades; it's about doing your personal best and giving your all to an assignment, a class, and a major! (And yes, I agree, we did just have another *Full House* moment.)

ACCORDING TO SOME PRETTY INTELLIGENT PEOPLE, EDUCATION IS . . .

One of the few things a person is willing to pay for and not get.

—WILLIAM LOWE BRYAN (1860-1956), PROFESSOR

Hanging around until you've caught on.

—ROBERT FROST (1874-1963), POET

One of the chief obstacles to intelligence and freedom of thought.

—BERTRAND A. RUSSELL (1872-1970), ENGLISH PHILOSOPHER, MATHEMATICIAN, AND WRITER

A form of self-delusion.

—ELBERT HUBBARD (1856-1915), AMERICAN AUTHOR,

EDITOR, AND PRINTER

[A process] which makes one rogue cleverer than another.

—OSCAR WILDE (1856-1900), BRITISH POET AND DRAMATIST

MAKING A GREAT START AT A COLLEGE EDUCATION
(A look at the basic elements you will need to be successful at learning)

GETTING STARTED
(Because what you do at the start can put you on a path toward success)

When it comes to being smart about your college education, the first week of college is very important—I'm talking "seat belt" important. And just so you know, I'm not talking about the first week of classes necessarily; I'm talking about those four, five, or six days you're on campus *before* you begin getting up at the butt-crack of dawn for your classes. So following this paragraph you're reading right now, a bunch of other paragraphs will begin that will help you know what you'll need to do to make sure you've done all you can to avoid big "class" problems later on. As with many other topics in this book, you will need to check with your college about their official procedures before you do anything. (And between you and me, sometimes it's the "procedures" that end up being the BIG problem.)

THE FIRST-WEEK TO-DO LIST

1. TALK TO YOUR ADVISOR. No matter if you've already registered, you will want to meet your advisor anyway. Right now, you might be thinking, *Why do I need to meet with my advisor?* Well, here's a quick rundown on why:

- **ADVISOR RULE #1: YOU WANT TO BUILD A GOOD RELATIONSHIP WITH HIM OR HER.** You want your advisor to know your face and your name. Think *Cheers*. When you need class information, you do not want to feel like you're talking to a stranger each time you contact your advisor. And at certain colleges, because of their large size or limited staffing or the number of students given to each advisor, getting to know your advisor can be a difficult task. But nonetheless, meet with her, build a relationship with her, tell her she's beautiful. That last part is a joke.

- **ADVISOR RULE #2: FIND OUT IF YOUR ADVISOR WILL BE WITH YOU THROUGHOUT YOUR COLLEGE EXPERIENCE.** If you have not yet declared a major, many colleges will simply assign you to a "this student does not have a clue about where he's going in life" advisor until you decide. It's good to know if your advisor will be temporary. You certainly don't want to be kissing up to an advisor who is going to leave you eventually, do you?

- **ADVISOR RULE #3: LASTLY, IF YOUR ADVISOR IS GOING TO BE WITH YOU LONG TERM, DOES SHE KNOW ANYTHING ABOUT YOUR MAJOR?** Surprisingly, some universities actually put students with advisors long term regardless of whether or not they know a student's major. If you believe your advisor knows too little about your major, then you will likely want to change advisors. You can choose to make this change right away or after you meet a few of the professors within your major. That's up to you. But securing an advisor within your major is a very smart decision, because advisors are usually connected, can help you get an internship or job, and can hook you up with many other collegiate benefits.

2. MAKE SURE YOU'RE SIGNED UP FOR THE CORRECT CLASSES. When you have that little conversation with your advisor, be sure to go over your class load with him or her. Unless you're 100 percent sure about what you're going to major in, ask your advisor to help you ensure that every class you are scheduled for is a general requirement—meaning, it's a class that is needed for all majors. I'm pretty sure you don't want to waste time taking a class that might not be useful.

3. GET SOME INFORMATION ABOUT YOUR PROFESSORS. Most colleges and universities have several different professors who teach the classes you will be taking, especially when you're a freshman. Find out what the "rumors" are regarding your professor's teaching style. You can ask your RA or any other upperclassman on campus. Or you can find a wealth of information about most professors online at RateMyProfessor.com.

4. BE SURE THAT YOUR CLASS SCHEDULE WORKS BEST FOR YOUR SCHEDULE. If at all possible, you want to have a class schedule that works *for* you and not against you. Some of you may want to take all of your classes on Tuesdays and Thursdays before noon so you can work on Monday, Wednesday, and Friday. If you're somewhat unmotivated in the morning, do not schedule a class for 7:30 a.m. You will be prone to skip. Of course, since you're a freshman, you're low on the totem pole and may not get that privilege (the higher the level you are in school, the sooner you get to choose your classes). But, if you pay attention to the registration schedule and get on the boat early, you may get your way.

THE FIRST-WEEK CHECKLIST: A FEW THINGS YOU MIGHT NEED TO DO BEFORE CLASSES BEGIN

[ ] Locate your classrooms

[ ] Purchase a daily planner to use only for classes

[ ] Locate the nearest library to your dorm

[ ] If it's not possible for you to have a laptop, locate the closest computer lab

[ ] Buy all of your books for classes, unless you did this during the summer

[ ] Make sure you have all of your needed college supplies—the basics, like paper and pens

When you have checked and made sure all of the above are completed, you should feel logistically ready for classes to begin. And being prepared logistically will indeed help you be ready emotionally, too. With no big logistics to worry about, you will be able to concentrate on what's important—getting an education.

YOUR PROFESSORS

(Because creating a good relationship with your professor will help you)

When I was a kid, I loved going to the Smithsonian Institution in Washington, D.C. On occasion my school would take field trips to the museum. Once, my class of twenty went to the National Museum of Natural History located in the Smithsonian. My seventh-grade teacher had arranged for us to have a guided tour of the dead, stuffed animals that filled the exhibits. Our *tour guide*, a very attractive twenty-eight-year-old Asian woman, was a bona fide "dead, stuffed animal" genius. Her knowledge about the animals left me amazed. Hearing that lady converse intelligently about all things four legged made me think, "I want to marry someone just like her." I stood there imagining how much fun it would be to sit around and talk with a woman about why the dodo bird became extinct. Back then, that kind of conversation would have been heavenly—yes, I was a nerd.

As all the kids stood around in a large circle waiting to enter the exhibit, our tour guide got very serious for a moment. She looked at us and said, "Kids, I want you to remember one thing; I am only a *guide* of the tour. If you want to really learn something, make sure you're experiencing the exhibit for yourself and not simply through my eyes." At that moment, one of the thirteen-year-olds who was in my class—he had failed a year—looked at me and said, "I don't know about you, but I'd like to experience her exhibits." But because I was a good Christian kid and, just maybe, didn't understand what he meant, I didn't laugh at his sexual joke. But my friend's (somewhat funny) joke didn't keep me from learning something new that day.

Despite the fact that I was only twelve, the tour guide's statement—the "you need to experience this museum for yourself" talk—struck me as moderately profound. And over the years, it hasn't simply been pertinent to that experience in the museum, but also to life in high school, college, and work, too. The people who guide you through life cannot force you to experience or to learn; you have to be willing to engage in that process for yourself.

Your professor is much like a tour guide. She can guide you through your class, but she can't *make* you fully experience the class or the topic unless you're willing to give of yourself. In other words, she can tell you facts. She can teach you equations. She can mark your research papers with red ink. She can bring you new insight to topics and thoughts. But just like us middle-school kids learned from that museum's cute tour guide, people must be willing to passionately jump into life (college included) and not depend on other people (like your professor) to be the extent of their experience. Unless you're willing to make an effort to engage and experience the class, you will not end up learning everything possible. In other words, you cannot depend on a professor to be the center of your learning experience while at college. If you do, you're only limiting yourself and the overall educational experience.

All professors are different. Some will become your best friends. Some will be so standoffish that you'll wonder if they have souls. Some will be overzealous about their subjects. And some are simply there because it pays the bills. How you enter the classroom will determine the student/professor relationship that develops over the course of the semester. And that relationship is important.

It's a must that you walk into any classroom eager to learn and ready to experience the subject not only through your professor's knowledge, but also through your personal investment in the class. Resist the urge to simply "get through" the class. Even if a class is not a part of your core major, don't discount it. Your professor will pick up on your interest (or as the case may be, lack of interest). When you begin classes, you will realize quickly that the relationships and interactions that you have with your professors will be the blood that pumps inside the veins of your education.

And investing yourself in a class you don't care for can be most difficult. One of the classes that I had to take when I was at Belmont University was American Literature. As a business major, I thoroughly believed that this class was a waste of my time. And to make matters worse, my professor was *way* more excited about *Leaves of Grass* and *The Great Gatsby* than I believed any individual ought to be. But despite my feelings about the class and my teacher's tendency to get too aroused when he spoke about Thoreau, I invested myself in the experience of learning as much as I could about American Literature. And that professor eventually became one of my favorites at college. And, I'm now a writer and not a corporate CEO, so that's gotta say something.

Good "professor tactics" are hard to identify. However, there are a few simple and basic guidelines that you can follow:

BASIC PRINCIPLES FOR GETTING ON YOUR PROFESSOR'S GOOD SIDE

1. BE FIVE MINUTES EARLY FOR CLASS. This shows respect not only to your professor, but also to the other students.

2. MAKE CONTACT WITH YOUR PROFESSOR IF YOU'RE SKIPPING CLASS. If you're not going to show up for a class, tell your professor ahead of time. Send him an e-mail or call his office.

3. READ THE SYLLABUS. Many of the questions you have about your professor and the class are answered there in black and white.

4. ANSWER AND ASK QUESTIONS. Be involved. Push past your fear of being wrong, and raise your hand once in a while. Asking and answering questions reveals your interest in the topic and class. (In high school, it's usually not cool to act like you're interested. But learning, and wanting to learn, are cool in college. Really!)

5. LEARN YOUR PROFESSOR'S LIKES AND DISLIKES. What kind of conversations does he encourage in class? How does he test? Does she like opinionated people? What does he respond well to in essays? Where is she from? Learning to anticipate and act on each professor's individual expectations is an almost-guaranteed better grade.

6. DO THE READING AND THE ASSIGNMENTS. Some of you, and you know who you are, will struggle with this throughout your college experience. But you're not in high school anymore. And a professor will not tolerate laziness.

7. LEARN FROM CORRECTION. Don't be one of those students who challenges every correction a professor makes on a paper or assignment. This kind of behavior only shows your lack of respect for the professor and the inability to take criticism.

8. ACT LIKE A GROWN-UP. Don't make silly excuses to your professor about why you failed to finish an assignment. Be straightforward, and they will usually be straightforward with you.

9. GET HELP IF YOU'RE HAVING TROUBLE. If you're struggling with a class, it's your responsibility to get help. Some professors will not make an effort to connect with failing students. So talk to your professor, get a tutor, or find a study group if you're having trouble. If you make the effort, your professor might just be impressed with your fervor to know the topic at hand. Remember, the *power* is in your hands. *Don't you just love the thought of responsibility?*

SIX QUESTIONS OR STATEMENTS YOU SHOULD ALMOST NEVER ASK OR SAY TO YOUR PROFESSOR

1. WILL THIS INFORMATION BE ON THE TEST? Professors hate this question. So do yourself a favor, and just assume whatever your professor talks about in class is fair game for testing. Usually, if your professor is talking about something meaningless to the subject or to testing, he will preface his "story" with "You won't be tested on this. . . ." But if you don't hear him say that, just assume. Of course, I know what "assuming" does, but I also know what asking ridiculous questions does.

2. CAN I CALL YOU AT YOUR HOME? *Yikes.* Most likely, a professor will put his or her "calling" guidelines in your syllabus or tell you the appropriate way in which to get in touch. If the information is not listed, *assume* it's off-limits (unless you've been given special permission). But please, *never* look up a professor's number in the phone book and call. That's highly unprofessional and reeks of neediness.

3. HOW MUCH TIME SHOULD I SPEND STUDYING FOR THIS EXAM? This question demonstrates poor effort, or worse, no motivation. Just study as much as you need to study in order to understand the material.

4. I THINK YOU MIGHT BE MISTAKEN. . . . One time I made the mistake of saying this. I told my marketing professor that he was wrong about a company's product. "Oh, really," he said. "Well, Mr. Turner, I find it hard to believe that you would know more than I do about a company that I *own*." Oh, it was an awful scene. From that day on, every time he mentioned his company, he would then look at me, and say, "Do you agree with this, Mr. Turner, or should I call *my* office and double-check this information?" It was extremely embarrassing. So please, don't contradict your teacher in front of the class. I don't care how *right* you believe you are or how *wrong* you believe the teacher might be. It's never good to disrespect your college authority in a public setting.

5. WELL, THIS IS MY OPINION. . . . I made the mistake of saying this once, too. I will spare you the details. I'll just say this: I learned the hard way that my professor (and the other class members) did not care what I thought. On the other hand, some majors require opinion sharing, and some professors ask for your thoughts. If that's the case, by all means, speak up. The point here? Be shrewd in your interactions with professors and in classroom behavior.

6. WILL YOU BE LETTING US OUT OF CLASS EARLY TODAY OR TEACHING THE *ENTIRE* TIME? Do I really need to give an explanation to this one? I'll just say this: Don't ask this question.

LEARNING A THING OR TWO ABOUT YOUR PROFESSOR BY READING THE SYLLABUS

Sadly, like I stated earlier in this book, on my first day of college I didn't even know what my stats professor was talking about when she mentioned the word *syllabus.* However, I figured out rather quickly that the collections of stapled-together papers that my professors handed to me* on the first day of classes were going to be crucial to my classroom success. Your professor's educational DNA (his styles of teaching and testing) is quite often written all over his syllabus. Go ahead; see for yourselves. So with that theory in mind, here's a code to figuring out your professor just by taking a quick glance at the syllabus.

PROFESSOR TYPE #1. If the syllabus is longer than five pages, detailed down to the exact thoughts he wants you thinking on October 2, and organized to near perfection, it means . . .

---

* Because of the advancement of technology, some professors now put their class syllabus online.

- Your professor has a serious tendency toward creating some educational drama, and I'm not talking about the kind of drama you see at the movie theater, either. I'm talking "gloom and doom if you don't do the work" drama.

- He's apt to get overly animated and excited about hard test questions, long reading assignments, and scientific experiments.

- There's a good chance this type of professor will be fun, compelling, and compassionate.

PROFESSOR TYPE #2. If the syllabus is less than two pages long, is compiled of only brief instructions and basic topics the class will cover (instead of Professor #1's detailed schedule), and is filled with a great deal of white space, it means . . .

- Your professor will more than likely be a difficult tester.

- Her confidence might be misinterpreted as cockiness.

- Over time she'll become one of your favorite professors; her teaching style will be challenging, but you'll learn a great deal from her teaching style.

PROFESSOR TYPE #3. If the syllabus is cluttered, filled with meaningless information, and leaves a little too much up to your imagination, it means . . .

- Just what you think it means. This kind of professor, rather than keeping you awake during class with great discussions about absolute truth, might be more apt to make your head ache.

○ You're going to have to ask a lot of questions.

○ He might be a scatterbrain, but he'll be kind and most likely a little easier. Oh, and he's probably an adjunct.

FOUR VERSES FROM PROVERBS 23 THAT EVERY COLLEGE STUDENT SHOULD KNOW

Oh listen, dear child – become wise;
    point your life in the right direction. . . .
Listen with respect to the father who raised you,
    and when your mother grows old, don't neglect her.
Buy truth – don't sell it for love or money;
    buy wisdom, buy education, buy insight.
Parents rejoice when their children turn out well;
    wise children become proud parents. (verses 19,22-24)

LIFE IN THE CLASSROOM
(Because you'll spend a great deal of time in one)

COLLEGE CLASS EXPERIENCE

You'll notice the significant difference in the number of people in your classes versus what you're used to in high school. Depending on the class and even the school, class sizes can range from a dozen to hundreds of students. Don't let large classes intimidate you. Instead, embrace them as part of your college experience. "Pit classes," as large classes are also known, are typically (but not always) freshman requirements. More than likely, your class sizes will get smaller as you begin to take classes within your major or minor. Regardless of the size or topic of class, following these tips will help you to maximize your success in the classroom:

- **YOU WILL BE MORE ATTENTIVE IN THE FRONT ROW**, especially in a pit class. So buck up and sit in the front, or at least one of the first couple rows. Forget what I said at the beginning of this book; yes, the nerds and butt-kissers sit up front, but you can usually learn something from the nerds and the butt-kissers. Also, when you're up in front, you are less likely to miss something important.

- **SHOW UP AT LEAST FIVE MINUTES BEFORE CLASSES BEGIN.** Yes, I know I mentioned this earlier, but it's important. So I'll mention it again.

- **TAKE THOROUGH NOTES.** If you have never had to take extensive notes like those needed in college, talk to your professor, teacher's assistant, or RA about note-taking resources on campus. Many schools will offer free seminars or tutors that assist in strengthening your note-taking skills. And if your college doesn't offer any help, check out CollegeBoard.com.

- **FOLLOW THE CLASS GUIDELINES THAT ARE OUTLINED IN YOUR SYLLABUS.** This means, do the homework before coming to class, study for exams well in advance, and so on. Your professor may or may not discuss the reading in class, but you can bet that if it is required reading, it will probably show up on a quiz or exam someday.

- **YOUR CELL PHONE SHOULD NOT BE ON – EVER.** It is a disruption to your class, your professor, and you. If you need to have it on, have it on vibrate and quietly excuse yourself if you need to take a call, but my best advice is this: Never answer your phone during a lecture. Even if it is a large class, picking up your phone is never okay.

- **LEARN THE NAMES OF THE PEOPLE YOU SIT NEAR.** It is nice to make at least a few acquaintances when you are sitting next to the same few people several times a week. Come test time, these familiar faces will probably be willing to form a small study group.
- **BRING YOUR LAPTOP TO CLASS.** If your professor allows it, taking notes directly onto your laptop will help you stay organized, and your notes will always be legible. And you won't get those nasty hand cramps from writing, either. But make sure your laptop volume is muted so you will not disturb your professor's lecture.
- **AFTER EACH CLASS, TAKE FIFTEEN MINUTES TO REVIEW YOUR NOTES.** If you desire your studying to be simplified a little, take the time to review your notes on the same day that you take them. Taking even a few minutes to read through what you learned will help you retain a great deal of information.
- **THINK.** Remember when I said that it's important to come to class ready to experience the topic for yourself? Well, one of the ways you can do this is by making a point to *think* while you're listening to a professor give a lecture. I know; it seems rather obvious, but you'd be surprised how many students are not actively listening in class. Dr. Bob Kizlik, a professional on human habits, says this about thinking: "Think about what the teacher is saying BEFORE writing down anything. Writing down each word is a WASTE OF TIME. Reorganize in your mind what the teacher says, and then write it down. This way you will be connecting the teacher's words with HOW you think. If you do this, your notes will make a lot more sense later on."[3]

PRACTICAL ADVICE FOR EDUCATION

Some believe it is scientifically proven that listening to classical music like Beethoven or Bach will help you concentrate while studying. A healthy supply of this style of music is available on iTunes, so you might want to give it a listen. I have actually tried this, and it really does seem to work.

STUDYING*
(Because you'll spend more time doing this than actually taking a class, and it's not that much fun)

- -

I hated studying; my mind was easily led astray while trying to study in college. It didn't take much, either. Noises bothered me. People walking around in the library distracted me. Flies sitting up on the ceiling often interested me more than studying the material. But if you want to be successful in your classes, it's imperative that you learn productive study habits. Not every study tip works with every kind of personality. So knowing how you best retain and learn information will be extremely important. Basically, this comes down to knowing yourself. Are you easily distracted? Do you study better with other people or alone? Do you need to have things repeated over and over again before you retain the information? Knowing the answers to these questions will help you design a college studying plan that works for you. Because admit it; there are other ways you'd rather spend your time. Here are a few basic study helps; you should, umm, *study* these.

---

* Countless study ideas exist. So, make sure you talk with your professor or TA about the "study help" resources available at your college.

PLAN AHEAD. First, before anything, buy a daily planner for college (try the TH1NK student planner). One of the most important keys to studying is actually strategizing your time in advance. As your professors give you assignments, write them down in your planner. Also, most reading assignments are already listed in your syllabus. You will find it quite helpful if you put that information in your planner. Yes, you can use your computer calendar, but I recommend buying a schedule that you can carry with you in your book bag. You're more apt to write assignments down on a tangible calendar, especially if your computer is turned off.

MAKE YOUR TIME COUNT. Plan out each week in hourly increments. This might be hard at first, but if you dedicate yourself to doing this, you'll actually end up having more time to study *and* to have fun. It's all about having a plan. When you plan your time, you will always be able to know when you're available to do something "extracurricular" or when you'll be in the library working on a research paper. Also, a schedule will help you avoid becoming overloaded with a bunch of all-nighters.

STUDY WHEN YOU'LL BE AT YOUR BEST. The last thing you want to do is make a habit of studying when you're tired and run-down. That's why a schedule is important; it will help you to create blocks of *good* studying time. Some people are good at night, and others are better in the morning. Again, you need to know what works best for you. Then, plan it, and stick to your plan.

USE YOUR TIME EFFECTIVELY. That really smart guy I quoted earlier, Dr. Bob Kizlik, has this to say about using our time: "Time is the most valuable resource a student has. It is also one of the most wasted of resources. The schedule you develop should guide you in how to allocate the available time in the most productive manner. Sticking to your schedule can be tough. Don't dribble away valuable time. Avoiding study is the easiest thing in the world. It's up to you to follow the schedule you prepared. A good deal of your success in high school or college depends on this simple truth."[4] For the record, I agree with this smart guy.

STUDY IN AN ENVIRONMENT THAT WORKS FOR YOU. If you are diagnosed or self-diagnosed ADHD, you should probably avoid studying at

Starbucks. However, if you process information verbally, get together with a study partner. Know which environment fosters concentration for you, and choose it.

PRACTICAL ADVICE FOR EDUCATION

As soon as next semester's class schedule is available, make sure you begin right away to try and figure out the classes you will want to take. Upon looking over the available classes, be sure to set up an appointment with your advisor. Your school will let you know when it's time to actually register, so keep your eyes and ears open.

EXTRA CREDIT: SOME ADVICE FROM FORMER COLLEGE STUDENTS FOR MAKING THE MOST OF YOUR EDUCATION . . .

I recommend visiting your professor once every couple of weeks during his or her office hours. This gives you a chance to get to know the real person behind all of that knowledge. I built some very good relationships with a couple of my professors, and now their names appear on my resume. I don't think that would have happened if I had not gotten to know them a little outside of the classroom.

—Ted, 25, Lee University

I had trouble with writing research papers when I went to college. So I visited the writing center on my campus, and they really helped me develop into a solid writer. I had no clue how much I would need to learn good communication skills. And today, I would not be nearly as articulate without the help of those "writing" volunteers. If your school offers a writing help center, go use it!

—Samantha, 34, Seattle University

The best part of my education was through internships. I think I learned more by doing than I ever did in the classroom. If your college offers an internship program, get involved as soon as you can. A good internship will teach you the skills you need to survive in the workplace.

— KAREN, 26, LIPSCOMB UNIVERSITY

Don't be afraid to ask for help. If you're struggling in a class or with a particular concept, go and get help. If you don't communicate your struggle to the professor or TA, they can't help you.

— SIMON, 30, BAYLOR UNIVERSITY

THREE IDEAS TO CONSIDER IF YOU REALLY LOVE LEARNING

○ BECOME A SPEED-READER. You may not know this, but you can actually learn to read faster and better. Although this type of class or product can be expensive, for many, it really works.

○ TAKE A COURSE ON STUDYING. Some schools actually offer classes meant to help you learn how to study. In most cases, you do not get credit for this class, but students who have taken this type of class say that they developed some very practical skills that helped them become more complete students.

○ BECOME A TUTOR. Because you will be helping students from many different types of studies, tutoring is a great way to learn. Usually, the best skill to tutor is writing. Of course, you need to be a good writer *before* you become a tutor. This is a great way to help other students and it's also an effective way to find a date. Don't judge me; you've seen those movies, too.

A PERSONAL STORY FROM THE AUTHOR

For years, I struggled to learn, study, and focus in a classroom setting. Throughout my childhood, everything from my test scores to my lack of concentration in classes revealed this. Throughout high school and college, it never occurred to me that I might have a condition that was actually keeping me from fully experiencing an education. Several years after college, because of an inability to concentrate on my work, I humbled myself enough to go and see a doctor about my inability to stay focused. After explaining to him what I was experiencing, he said it sounded like I might have ADHD (Attention-Deficit/Hyperactivity Disorder).

When I first heard my doctor's diagnosis, I was scared. Like most people, I didn't want to be labeled. By this time in my life, I had expected that I might have a form of adult ADHD. Just like you, I had seen the commercials. In order to be sure about his diagnosis, my doctor wanted me to get a second opinion. So he sent me to a psychiatrist. After talking to the psychiatrist, he was certain that I had ADHD.

I write this because I know that some of you are struggling to learn, too. You can't concentrate. You have trouble studying. And you feel like you waste a lot of time. There is help for ADHD and other forms of learning disabilities. Sometimes the help comes in the form of medication, and sometimes it's through exercises or classes or therapy. You need to talk with your parents and your doctor about what is best for you.

If you think you might have ADHD, don't be embarrassed by it. But don't let it be a crutch, either. Learn all you can about your own particular need. Talk to your parents and doctor about how you're feeling. And together, you can make a wise decision about your situation. For more information about ADHD, visit www.chadd.org/.

THE CONCLUDING LIST

Write these five things from chapter 4 on a sheet of paper and pretend it's a cheat sheet; and then pull it out during tests. (Man, I'm pretty impressed with myself. I think this chapter on education is really good. If you hated it, pretend I *didn't* include my e-mail address at the beginning of this book.)

1. BECOME A SPEED-READER. For some reason, speed-readers are cool to me. I think you should be cool!

2. CREATE GOOD STUDY HABITS. Don't be one of those students who simply glide through school without breaking open a book; that's just not cool. (See the final sentence of point 1.)

3. DON'T CALL YOUR PROFESSOR AT HOME. Unless he says it's okay. However, don't take that one time as a license to call whenever you want. You don't want your professor feeling icky about you. And he will—if you call ALL THE TIME.

4. DO YOU KNOW THE DEFINITION OF SYLLABUS? Write it here: This will save me from having to write it here again.

5. MAKE EVERY CLASS COUNT. You wouldn't think of doing anything less, right? Yeah, I know I say "right" a lot. Give a guy a break.

NOTHING GREAT IN THE WORLD HAS BEEN
ACCOMPLISHED WITHOUT PASSION.

– GEORG WILHELM FRIEDRICH HEGEL, GERMAN INVENTOR

CHAPTER 5

WELLNESS

(Despite what you've been told, being sick at college is not that much fun, eating healthy is always a good thing, exercise is good, too, and emotional wellness makes everything better!)

The concept of total wellness recognizes that our every thought, word, and behavior affects our greater health and well-being. And we, in turn, are affected not only emotionally but also physically and spiritually.
— GREG ANDERSON

WHEN I WAS A junior in college, I contracted mono after swimming in one of the college public pools. For three weeks, my head hurt so badly I couldn't sit up, my throat was so sore and enflamed that I couldn't swallow a pill, and because of a bad reaction to some prescribed antibiotics, hallucinations and restlessness prevailed. Needless to say, my symptoms left me pretty much unable to function as a student at college.

I missed two weeks of classes.

I missed all of my finals except one.

I missed three weeks of my internship.

I didn't get to hang out with any of my friends.

And the worst of it was, my mother was nowhere around to take care of me. It was hard being sick without my mother's tender love and care. She was eight hundred miles away from me and was quite worried about how I was feeling. Throughout being sick though, my mother called me five times a day to find out how I was feeling. And she did this by asking me a thousand questions.

"Are you drinking plenty of fluids?" she asked me during one of our many conversations.

"Yes, I am."

"Is your room clean, Matthew? You need to make sure that you're not just sitting in your own germs or you won't get any better."

"I'm too sick to clean, Mom."

"Are you taking your antibiotics?"

"Yes."

"Are you getting plenty of sleep?"

"I think so."

"Have you talked to your doctor lately?"

"Not since Tuesday."

"What did he say?"

"I can hardly remember."

"Are you feeling better than yesterday? Are your glands swollen? Do you still have a fever? Are you getting sick of me calling?"

"No. Yes. Yes. Maybe a little but I still love you."

Can you relate? You probably can. Most moms, if they care even a little, will ask their sick kids a hundred questions, hoping some of the answers would put their minds at ease. *Why?* Because they're concerned, worried, and perhaps just a little overbearing about your health, safety, and overall well-being. That's just what moms do. I think "worrying about your wellness" is actually a part of a mom's job description. And I'll be honest with you; your mom's worry is apt to get a little more intense when you go away for college.

But moms have a reason to worry a little. Your overall wellness is extremely important. And moms usually know this.

PRACTICAL ADVICE FOR STUDENTS ABOUT WELLNESS

If you get sick (only minor sicknesses apply here, like the stomach flu or the common cold) when you're at college, don't forget to . . .

. . . drink your fluids. Well, not *your* fluids, but fluids (OJ, water, and perhaps V8)

. . . get some rest (being sick offers the only time it's kosher to skip class)

. . . call your mom (if she hasn't already called and annoyed you)

. . . ask your mom what you should do (she's dying to tell you anyway)

. . . go see the doctor if your illness lasts longer than 48 hours without improvement (get one of your new friends to take you)

. . . take your insurance card with you if you go to the doctor

YOU AND WELLNESS

Unless you're a hypochondriac,* it's quite likely that your parents will be a great deal more concerned for your college wellness (health, nutrition, safety, and the like) than you will be. I don't mean to stereotype, but face it; good wellness practices are not often the first priority of college students.

In fact, if you're like the average college student (and not all of you are), when it comes to your health, you sometimes tend to be a little inconsiderate. Just in case you weren't paying attention, I just basically

---

* A pretty big word that means nothing to you unless you've been diagnosed as one of them.

implied that, despite caring about your complexion, how good (or bad) you look in a bathing suit, and the fashion statement your college apparel choices are making, you're still apt to not take very good care of yourself while at college. Now, I know you don't necessarily *mean* to be insensitive toward your personal *self*. But face it; when it comes to things like your body; physical, emotional, and mental health; personal security; and spiritual wellness, many of you are a little more like Mary Kate and Ashley than you are like the Dalai Lama.

I'm going to assume (perhaps a little prematurely) that you haven't spent too much time contemplating college and how it might affect your personal health and safety. Sure you've probably had a few conversations about weight gain or homesickness, but other than a few conversations about the normal college worries, a plan for personal wellness is not something most college students usually spend a ton of time thinking about.

However, for your personal *wholeness*, I believe it will be important for you to spend a little time on a regular basis strategizing your personal plan for wellness. Of course, you don't have to go overboard. To be considered aware of your personal health and safety while at college doesn't mean you have to become an obsessive-compulsive overspiritualized health guru. It just means you have to be smart about the health and safety challenges that college might bring.

You need to participate in managing, maintaining, and pursuing your own personal college wellness. In other words, it's important that you become informed about wellness. When you're informed, you'll have the information you need to make good choices that will only make your college experience better. (And it might keep you from gaining the freshman fifteen, too!)

PRACTICAL ADVICE FOR STUDENTS ABOUT WELLNESS

If you're one of the many college students who struggle with minor eating disorders, food addictions, or obesity, many colleges offer help. Today, most colleges employ on-campus nutritionists to help you create a plan for healthy eating within a confidential relationship. Many colleges also offer counseling for such conditions, too. Visit the student life office on your campus to find out if your college offers such services.* If not, talk to your medical doctor about helping you create an effective eating plan for your individual lifestyle.

HALF A VERSE FROM PROVERBS 17 THAT EVERY COLLEGE STUDENT SHOULD KNOW

A cheerful disposition is good for your health. (verse 22)

---

* Make sure you also find out if there's a cost involved with this service. You know with college, there always seems to be a cost.

A FEW GOOD IDEAS TO HELP YOU LIVE THE GOOD (AND HEALTHY) LIFE WHILE AT COLLEGE

- -

FOOD

(Because food just might become your worst enemy while at college)

When it comes to food and the campus life, I find it very ironic that college students often gain weight their first year. I'm sure you've heard about the dreaded freshmen fifteen (I've already mentioned this cliché twice in this book). And although most students believe that the "fifteen" pounds are gained within the first year, many times it actually happens in the first semester.

But what I find ironic is that many freshmen gain weight despite frequent complaints that the cafeteria food tastes like a bowel movement from Satan. So with that in mind, I have come up with two assumptions to explain how the weight gain happens: (1) either freshmen learn to enjoy the flavor of Satan's poo and eat a lot of it, or (2) they end up spending a lot of money by getting their nutrition (or lack of nutrition) elsewhere.

I'm not going to go into a long diatribe on the benefits of eating healthy, well-balanced meals. You know the benefits. In fact, you've been force-fed the benefits of eating healthily since you were a kid. Because of this, I'm assuming you know that fruits, vegetables, protein, fiber, and dairy are all very important parts of the healthy food equation. And by knowing this, you are probably also well aware that it's important for you to get a certain amount of "healthy" servings a day. But just like it's sometimes difficult to eat right when you're at home, it will no doubt be even harder to eat healthily at school. Despite it being hard, if you want to eat the kinds of food that help you succeed in school and sports, it's possible. But you have to want it. If you don't make it a priority, then you'll end up creating bad habits quickly.

Despite cafeteria food often tasting bad and being less than fabulous *for* you, it's *still* possible to make good and healthy food choices.

Here are a few eating survival suggestions. This is not an exhaustive list. For more information on eating healthy, visit Ediets.com.

1. ALWAYS EAT BREAKFAST. You've heard it a thousand times — breakfast is the most important meal you can eat. Sadly, breakfast is also the easiest meal to skip. Eating a well-balanced meal in the morning will help you be more alert during classes. Of course, you don't need to eat pancakes, bacon, and biscuits every morning; you'll certainly gain weight if you do that. Eat a bowl of *healthy* cereal with a banana (Reese's Peanut Butter Cereal doesn't count!). Or chomp down a granola bar and drink a glass of milk. No matter what your morning eating habits were before college, get into the habit of eating a good breakfast.

2. CARRY HEALTHY SNACK OPTIONS WITH YOU. Put a couple of power bars or an apple in your book bag. Having a good, healthy snack along with you will help you resist the temptation of buying an unhealthy food option when you're hungry and in a hurry, and this will also help you not overeat at lunch or dinner.

3. PORTIONS ARE EVERYTHING. Eating the cafeteria mashed potatoes with gravy is not the worst thing in the world, but eating a thousand calories' worth of mashed potatoes and gravy three times a week might just kill you. If you choose to eat cafeteria foods that are filled with fat, cholesterol, and calories, then make sure your portions are small and that you don't go back for seconds. Those second trips to the food line will add inches to your waistline and unhealthy resistance for your arteries.

4. VARIETY IS GOOD. Don't eat all meats or all carbs. And make sure you're getting a healthy amount of uncooked fruits and veggies. When you're at college, this is pretty simple. Most schools have salad bars and selections of fruits made available daily. Just remember that *uncooked* is key. Most cooked vegetables at college have zero nutrients and are filled with sodium and fat. You might as well suck on a salt lick.

5. ONE SODA A DAY. College students drink a ton of soda. Soda is nothing but flavored sugar water. And sadly, sugar offers you nothing but empty calories. I wish it weren't true. Just remember that for every cup (eight ounces) of soda you drink, you are consuming one hundred calories. Think about that the next time you drink a forty-four-ounce Big Gulp of Coke from 7-Eleven. If you must have a little flavor with your drink, go with natural fruit juices instead. The calories are still there, but natural sugars are much better for you than unnatural.

6. DRINK WATER, LOTS OF IT. Carry a bottle of water with you everywhere you go. Drink at least forty-four ounces of water daily. That's one Big Gulp of water. The best option is to try to wean yourself completely off soda and become a bona fide water drinker, although I realize this may not be fully realistic. I dare you: Drink only water for two weeks straight, and see how much you crave soda after that two weeks. You'll be pleasantly surprised.

7. ALCOHOL CONSUMPTION IS VERY FATTENING. For most of you, it's illegal to be drinking alcoholic beverages anyway. So this *should* be easy for you. However, if you make the stupid choice to break the law, you're consuming a ton of calories. They don't call it the "beer belly" for nothing. (I'll talk more about alcohol later.)

8. THE SALAD BAR CAN BE GOOD AND BAD. When you eat from the salad bar (which you should as often as you can stand it), don't drown your salad in ranch dressing. Dressing is one of the most fattening foods available. Instead, fill a small cup with your dressing of choice and dip your fork into the dressing, then into your salad. You'll still get the taste but will avoid the unbelievable amount of calories. Or, if you're hard-core, you can also eat your salad plain. That's the best option. Also, stay away from potato salad, coleslaw, and other mayo-based "salads." They're pretty much lard with flavor.

9. AVOID EATING AFTER 8:00 P.M. Often college students get into the habit of eating late and right before bedtime. This is the *worst* thing you can do if you're trying to keep off the pounds. When you eat late at night, your body has no time to burn those calories. You end up going to bed completely full and instead of burning some of what you eat, your body consumes it. If you do feel hungry before bedtime, eat something light like a small bowl of cereal.

10. DON'T DO WHAT YOUR FRIENDS DO. You *will* meet people at college with horrible eating habits. And you'll be tempted to copy what you see them do. Flee from temptation! Tell them to get behind you. Stand on the Word of God and be made strong. Well, I'm going a little overboard; you don't have to get all Pentecostal on your new friends. But it would be best if you avoided making their poor eating habits your own.

When you're at college, food often becomes a part of everything you do. From studying to watching TV to going to see a movie or a simple Friday-night gathering, food somehow becomes a part of nearly every college lifestyle component. Look for opportunities to do things where food is not the focus. Or make the food option healthier. For example, on a movie night, serving lower-fat popcorn instead of "Movie Theater Triple Butter!" popcorn is a much better decision, and one that's not too difficult to make.

Your success in eating well at college will depend upon how you think about food. If you plan ahead to make wise choices about your food consumption, you will be more likely to make good decisions when walking through the cafeteria line. Even though most of the food is bad, the cafeteria serves a ton of variety and the ability to go back to the food line again and again. Trust me; it's easier than you think to consume 1,500 calories in one sitting. (If you're not food-savvy, 1,500 calories is *a lot*. The average person isn't supposed to eat more than 2,000 calories in a *day*.)

EATING WELL AT COLLEGE IS GUARANTEED TO . . .

. . . make you more alert in your classes

. . . make you feel better about yourself

. . . give you the energy you need for sports, working out, and other activities

. . . help keep your complexion free of acne

. . . keep you regular (and regular is good)

. . . keep you fit and firm

. . . help you focus on studying and research papers

SEVEN WELL-LOVED COLLEGE FOODS YOU SHOULD CONSUME IN MODERATION

1. POTATO CHIPS. Often considered the worst food for you, potato chips are high in fat, calories, and sodium. If you're craving a salty snack, try lower-calorie and less-fattening baked potato chips or pretzels.

2. ICE CREAM. The 98 grams of fat and 1,960 calories in a half-gallon of plain Breyer's vanilla ice cream will be a detriment to your desire for a thin waistline. And don't even get me started on Ben and Jerry's. That stuff is a killer. Instead, try eating Italian ice. Sure, it has calories, but it doesn't have the fat.

3. PIZZA. Although all your friends will get into the craze of ordering pizza every night at 10:00 p.m., don't join their insanity! Obviously, once in a while won't kill you. But some college students literally eat pizza on an almost-daily basis (because it's tasty and very cheap in college towns).

4. POPCORN. Unless the popcorn you buy contains no salt and no butter, then it would be a good plan to avoid the fat, sodium, and calories of movie theater and microwave popcorn. Instead, eat puffed wheat patties. I'm kidding; just buy the healthier versions of popcorn.

5. FAST FOOD. It doesn't matter if it's McDonald's, Burger King, Wendy's, Sonic, or any other restaurant establishment with a mascot, a "play-land," or wrapped-up sandwiches; you would be doing yourself a favor to not get into the habit of visiting fast-food restaurants.

6. BEER. Even the most conservative of Christian college students might struggle with the party scene. On top of beer being an illegal substance for college freshmen, it's also *really* unhealthy.

7. CANDY. No matter if it's chocolate or fruit-flavored, candy is nothing but processed sugar. Even the candy that says "fat free" is probably high in calories. You don't have to avoid candy like it's the plague, but it would be smart to eat it in moderation.

Of course, the list of bad-for-you foods could fill this book, but that would make it a very boring book. When it comes to eating, *moderation* is the most important lesson you can learn. Having pizza or popcorn or a candy bar is fine once in a while, but it's in making pizza an every-other-day habit that it becomes a problem. And sadly, a lot of college students have disgusting eating habits because they have never learned the art of moderation. Moderation is a good word for you to learn. In fact, why don't you go write it seventeen times in your journal. Okay, if you were actually getting my point, you would have replied, "No, I am only going to write it *five* times, because I believe in moderation." See how easy it can be? Just remember, "moderation" results vary by situation.

PRACTICAL ADVICE FOR STUDENTS ABOUT WELLNESS

According to the American Academy of Pediatrics (aap.org), if you have the following symptoms, you should get your butt to a doctor's office.

- If you have a fever of 102.5 degrees or higher (Have I told you lately that you're really hot?)

- If you have a headache accompanied by a stiff neck (I don't know why this combination is bad, but people smarter than I am say it is.)

- If you have pain with urination (Ouch!)

- If you have an unusual discharge from your penis or vagina, or if you have a significant change in your menstrual cycle (I don't know anything about this, and I'm okay with that.)

- If you have pain in the abdomen that will not go away (You're such a pain in the abdomen!)

- If you have a persistent cough, chest pain, or trouble breathing (I'm pretty sure this could mean you're dying.)

- If you have pain or any other symptoms that worry you or last longer than you think they should (Yeah, so you hypochondriacs should have a ball with this one.)

EXERCISE: LET'S GET PHYSICAL

(Because it's a habit that you need to develop [or keep] sooner rather than later)

Many of you already exercise. In fact, some of you are pretty much fanatics about exercising. Perhaps you were a high-school athlete or maybe you just do it to look good. Although vanity is usually not a good thing to possess, it can be a great motivator when it comes to exercising. Looking in the mirror and being confident about your body can give you confidence in all areas of life—including the classroom.

But now that you're going to college, keeping up with a regular exercise regimen might be difficult. The truth is, if you schedule your time right, there's plenty of time to work out in college. But you have to *make time* for it. For you fanatics, who are addicted to the gym, you won't have any trouble hitting the weight room and treadmill. But for those of you who simply exercise, not because it's an addiction but because it's the healthy thing to do, it will be imperative for you to schedule time to exercise.

For those of you who have never exercised a day in your life, it would be good for you to fit it in, too. Exercise is not only good for weight control; it also helps you stay alert, sleep better, and be more confident. Not to mention the internal health benefits that every doctor in the world can tell you about.

Every one of you knows the benefits of thirty minutes of exercise three times a week. Now that you're at college, you'll need to work at reaping those benefits. For those of you who love to exercise, just make sure you get into a regular routine once you're settled into classes. But for all of you who have long resisted the exercise urge, here are a few suggestions to help you get a little physical activity.

WALK TO CLASS. Don't take the bus to class. Yes, your campus is *huge*, but you will be too if you never walk. You're a big kid now; you'll be fine. Walking to class will help get your heart rate up and will also burn some of those calories you're consuming. A little trick: Never learn the bus schedule. If you don't know where and when the bus comes, the temptation to ride it will decrease substantially.

SKIP THE ELEVATOR. Take the stairs to the fifth floor instead.

STUDY AND WALK AT THE SAME TIME. Put some of your class notes onto a few three-by-five cards and study while you walk around the campus. Or if you can, record your notes into an MP3 format and listen to your notes. Actually, that's a brilliant idea, if I do say so myself!

MAKE ONE GOOD HABIT A MONTH. Try one new "active" thing a month. And no, making out with your significant other doesn't count. Perhaps it's doing fifty push-ups three times a week. Or maybe you can do some stretching while you're taking a shower. Look for opportunities to exercise throughout your day. Just avoid butt crunches during class. They can be very distracting.

TRY SOMETHING FUN. Many people think of exercise only as running or hitting the gym. And for some people, they would rather die than be caught on a stair-climber. If this is you, then find a way to make exercise fun. Go hiking. Play tennis. Swim twice a week. Join an intramural volleyball league. Join a pickup game of flag football. Just do something that will get your body moving and your heart pumping.

EMOTIONAL WELLNESS

(Because you never know what life might bring your way)

Wellness is more than simply eating good food and running on a tread-mill a few times a week. Indeed, it's a lot more. Much more important than doing things to improve your waistline is proactively engaging in habits and choices meant to fill you emotionally. To some, "emotional fulfillment" might seem like New Age mumbo jumbo. But people who invest wisely into the emotional parts of their being are often more complete individuals.

Your emotional wellness affects how you feel and think and react in situations (good and bad). People who are emotionally healthy are not people who never get upset or angry. However, they don't let their emotions (or how they feel) control them or define them.

Unfortunately, many think of emotions only as one's tendency to cry or to get upset. But more than simply your quickness to tear up during a sad movie or punch something when you're mad, the emotional part of you greatly affects how you love, serve, and bring peace to others. Your emotions even affect your response to criticism, direction, and disagreement. Emotions also play a huge role in your anger toward a person or situation, the depression you might feel when you're alone, and the stress that gets created when you're overwhelmed. When you begin to comprehend how extensively your emotions impact so many different areas of your life, it becomes evident why pursuing habits that promote emotional wellness is so important.

When you're finally comfortable in your college routine, it will become even more apparent to you why emotional wellness is important for college success. Often, some college students experience so much change that it tends to throw their emotions into frenzy. This often leads some to feel things that they have never felt before—like the inability to handle stress, bouts with depression and personal fear, and feelings of self-doubt and uncontrolled pain. No matter if you're emotionally healthy or not, it's quite possible to feel all of those things. But people who have an ongoing desire to pursue emotional wellness will be much less likely to become consumed by stress, pain, depression, or anxiety, or will know themselves well enough to realize the need for help.

But too often, a student faces extreme conditions unprepared. It's in these kinds of situations that the emotional becomes life-changing, devastating, and seemingly hopeless. This kind of event happens quicker than most believe. Consider the words of these two college students:

I was your everyday student. In high school, I got good grades, played several sports, and had well-defined relationships. People were quite impressed with me. For anyone who knew me, they probably thought I was an emotionally healthy person. But that masquerade ended pretty quickly when I went to college. Out of a deep need for male approval, which stemmed from a dysfunctional relationship with my father, I developed many unhealthy relationships with men. Throughout my freshman year, I jumped in and out of relationships quickly. Toward the end of that first year, one of those relationships developed into a long-term commitment. I dove headfirst into loving that guy. Little did I know, I had actually made him my life.

When I was a sophomore in college, he broke up with me. Unfortunately, that sent my emotions into a devastating tailspin. I became almost psychotic—like an out-of-control, hysterical mess. My emotions were in such disarray; I almost lost everything. Well, at least, that's what it felt like. With my mom far away, I didn't have a good support group around me. I had invested most of my time into my ex-boyfriend. Because I didn't have good community, that breakup poorly affected my grades, a few of my older friendships, and also an internship. This sounds ridiculous, but I ended up having to take a semester off to recover.

—Katie, 23, University of Idaho

College was hard right from the start for me. I actually lost my father to cancer when I was a senior in high school. When it happened, I appeared quite strong and secure. I put on a good spiritual face in front of my church. Figuring that God would eventually make me feel okay, I made a point to simply keep moving forward. Despite college only being a few months away, I told everyone I was ready, that I would be okay. I poured every bit of my emotion into getting prepared for college—that's what all of my friends told me I should do. It wasn't until February of my second semester that the weight of what had happened ten months before hit me like an avalanche. Having never felt depression before or even considered it an option for a Christian, I didn't know the signs. Slowly, over time, I began to realize that what I was feeling might be symptoms of depression. As much as I tried to keep what I was feeling from my family and friends, every one of them knew something was wrong. They could see it, not only in my anger, but they could see it in my lifestyle. Scared by the thought that I could be depressed, I resisted help at first. But what I was feeling was having an impact on how I viewed most of my life. In fact, everything I pursued seemed much bigger than I could handle at the time. I lived like that for four and a half months. It wasn't until I went home for the summer that an old high school friend of mine encouraged me to seek out help. That first conversation with my friend was the first time I actually said the words "depression" out loud.

—JEFFREY, 21, OLIVET NAZARENE UNIVERSITY

College gives one's emotions the room to breathe, the chance to be unprotected by the security found in family, church, and close friendships. If these emotions are avoided, feelings can certainly grow into something that can cause one to believe his or her life is falling apart. For Katie, college spawned an unmet childhood need (to have a good relationship with her father) to come to the surface. However, for Jeffrey, it was unfinished closure concerning the death of his dad that eventually fueled his emotions to break apart. The emotional backlash these two experienced might have been unavoidable, but it could have been limited.

You don't know how your emotions will respond to the situations you'll encounter while at college. For some, it doesn't take all that much to make them feel overwhelmed and anxious. For others, like Jeffrey and Katie, big circumstances will arise in your life, causing you pain or depression or feelings of hopelessness. But here's the deal: You can't make horrible situations go away, but you can proactively create lifestyle habits that support you emotionally, which will make these tough life happenings less able to control you and affect how you feel, react, and live.

SEVEN IDEAS FOR EMOTIONAL WELLNESS

1. THE TWO-PEOPLE IDEA. I believe you should have two people (prefer-ably the same sex as you) in your life who you trust. Make one a friend and make the other an older mentor who has lived more life than you. And don't pick just anyone. You want to respect these two people profession-ally, spiritually, and personally. Make a point to talk to these people on a regular basis. Spend time praying with them. Push yourself to be open and honest about how you feel. Having "two people" in your life will give you the ongoing opportunity to express your emotions. Whatever life brings, you'll already have a built-in support group ready to help you through.

2. JOURNAL. You should know the benefits of this by now. The continu-ous practice of writing down your thoughts (good and bad) will help you better process healing, pain, joy, and success.

3. TALK TO MOM AND DAD. If you have a relatively close relationship with your mother and father, it's almost always to your benefit to keep your parents aware of what is going on inside that head and heart of yours. In most cases, your mom and dad will be able to help you navigate your way through the ups and downs of life. Don't keep your troubled thoughts from your parents; remember, God has put them in your life for a reason.

4. SPIRITUAL INVESTMENT. Don't underestimate the influence of prayer, meditation on Scripture, and a faith-based community on your emotional health. A well-engaged soul finds great strength and peace when proactively allowing God to fill him up spiritually and emotionally. Also, a faith-based community is a great place for you to find an ongoing network of support.

5. PRE-EMPTIVE COUNSELING. Counseling is not just for those who are depressed or who are going through marriage woes. Even if you're not going through a life-changing, emotional battle, it might be good for you to talk to a counselor (clinical or pastoral) about the change that comes with going to college. This is especially important if you've recently experienced a painful circumstance like the death of a friend or family member, the divorce of your parents, or perhaps a serious illness. Even if you *think* you're fine, having a conversation with a trained counselor may help you avoid becoming overwhelmed with your personal life when at school.

6. DON'T CREATE UNNEEDED DRAMA. Unnecessary drama often steals precious time away from a person's life. So try not to create more of what you don't need. This action begins with *knowing* what you can and cannot handle. Do you become too emotionally involved in dating relationships too soon? Then make a point not to date in your first semester. Are you the type of person who gets overwhelmed by too much homework? Then take fifteen credits only—don't overload yourself with what you know will make you crazy. Once you have a defined concept of what you can or cannot handle, make good and healthy decisions accordingly.

7. GET HELP. Most important, if you begin to feel emotionally overwhelmed, be quick about finding the help you need. Go to your college's counseling center and talk to someone. Talk to your FCA, Campus Crusade for Christ, or Navigator leader. If you resist finding help, you will only get worse. It's very difficult to be successful at learning when you're consumed by your emotions.

SAFETY

Remember Smokey the Bear? He was all about teaching you fire safety. Well, during this next section, you can call me Safety the College Clown. I'll be teaching you about staying safe at college.

Safety is extremely important for all college students to think about. Proactively thinking about safety gives you the information needed to make good decisions about campus life. All campuses are different. Some colleges are located in places much safer than others. In other words, a school in Nebraska is going to have different safety concerns than one in Miami. So get to know your campus. Before you attend, you should talk with your student life office or security office concerning your campus's safety guidelines, crime history, and security personnel. Once you have the facts about your college's safety record, you can make better decisions about what precautions you'll need to take at campus.

Here's the deal: Many college students are a little naïve when they go off to college. It's okay; you can admit it. I was naïve, too, and because of *not knowing*, I made some pretty risky decisions about my personal safety. Fortunately, my decisions didn't end up hurting me too badly. But that's not true for everyone. Sadly, it's usually the silly, often avoidable mistakes that get people into unnecessary trouble.

Please know, I don't include this section in the book to make you scared; I simply think it's important that you go to college aware. Being aware can keep you safe, and in some instances, it can keep you alive. So take your personal safety seriously. No matter what school you go to, follow the rules below for your own good, but also to keep your mom from worrying too much!

BASIC PRINCIPLES TO KEEP SAFETY FIRST

1. NEVER WALK ALONE AFTER DARK. I don't care if you think your campus is as safe as Disney World; *never* walk anywhere on campus alone after dark. In fact, the bigger your group is the better (especially if you're women). But this rule isn't just for girls; it's for guys, too. Wherever you go, go together. There is no *good* excuse to walk alone at night. If you get into a situation where you are alone with no one to walk with you, call the cab company that your college has deemed safe or notify your campus security and they will assist you. Just don't risk being alone after dark, okay? Do it for me?

2. KNOW THE *SAFEST* ROUTE ACROSS CAMPUS. Study your campus. Map out your safest routes between classes and your dorm. Once you know the routes, locate every emergency telephone on your route. If you ever witness anything suspicious, use the phone. Even the silliest of assumptions is worth reporting.

3. FOLLOW THE DORM SAFETY RULES. Most colleges have dorm rules in place to provide you with a safe living environment. But these rules are good only when each individual enforces them. You should talk with your RA about ideas, questions, or concerns regarding dorm safety. Here are a couple rules that you should follow:

- **ALWAYS MAKE SURE THE DOOR CLOSES BEHIND YOU.** Most colleges have card or key-entry locks on all dormitory doors. Some schools keep these doors locked at all times and others only make the "key" necessary during evening and overnight hours. When you come in during locked hours, be sure to close the door behind you.
- **REPORT STRANGERS.** If there is someone running around the dorms who you don't believe belongs there, report him to your RA. It's always better to be overly safe.

4. ALWAYS CARRY "HELP" WITH YOU. Every time you leave your dorm, check to see if you have your cell phone, Mace or pepper spray, and a little bit of cash in case you need to get a cab or take the bus.

5. PROGRAM IMPORTANT NUMBERS INTO YOUR PHONE. Program the following numbers into your cell phone: 911, the non-emergency police line, the campus security phone line, the number to the "safe cab company," and the number of your RA.

6. LET SOMEONE YOU TRUST KNOW YOUR SCHEDULE. At least three people should know where you are at all times: your parents (give them your basic school schedule each semester), a good friend (exchange schedules with each other; make the other your "safety buddy"), and your RA.

7. WHEN LIGHTBULBS ACROSS CAMPUS ARE OUT, REPORT THEM. Campuses are big and sometimes college maintenance crews overlook burned-out lightbulbs on dorms, classroom buildings, and gymnasiums.

If you see a light that is out or flickering, contact your student life office. Also, if you notice a spot on campus where you believe more lighting is needed, make your request known. Yes, this is a little over-the-top, but when it comes to safety, every little bit of information helps.

For more information on safety and safety tips, go to SecurityOnCampus.org.

CAN YOU PASS THIS TWO-QUESTION TEST ABOUT PARTY SAFETY?
Don't Worry; It's Multiple Choice

SCENARIO #1

Sophia and a bunch of her good friends are at a college party. She's being good. She wouldn't think about drinking – well, maybe a little sip of Diet Coke now and then, but nothing that's going to compromise the eighteen-year-old's conservative Christian upbringing. Of course, she's a little bit sweaty because she's been dancing pretty hard to an old Britney tune for more time than she's comfortable admitting. (In fact, Sophia's too shy – and conservative – to admit that she's grown to like Ms. Spears over the years. Sure, she thinks the pop star's music is cheesy, but that doesn't stop her from shaking her backside a little when the deejay plays the to-die-for remix of "Toxic." She thinks to herself, "Hey, we've all got our weaknesses, right?) Suddenly, right in the middle of her performing the best dance move she ever stole from JLO, a stranger approaches her. But you see, this is not just *any* stranger; he's the best-looking stranger in the room. The very stranger Sophia's been eyeing all night long. She's been secretly hoping he would come over and talk to her. She watches him walk toward her, carrying a couple of drinks in his hands. She can't help but notice the gold cross necklace dangling around his thick, muscular neck. "Maybe he loves Jesus," she thinks. With the music pumping in the background, the hot stranger leans over and yells in Sophia's ear, "I got a drink here with your name on it." Sophia smiles at him and says, "Oh, that's okay; I don't drink." The stranger's grin sparkles, "Oh, neither do I; this is non-alcoholic. It's just a Diet Coke." Sophia smiles. "How did you know I like Diet Coke?" she asks. "I've been watching you all night long. So do you want it or am I going to be left here looking like a loser?"

STOP. How should Sophia reply? What should she say to the hot stranger? What would you say to him? Choose from the following responses:

   A: "That's so sweet of you. Of course I'll take the drink."
   B: "That's so sweet of you. But I'm not really thirsty. Maybe my friend would like it."
   C: "That's so sweet of you. But I don't want your stupid drink. I think you're lying to me. I think you've slipped some kind of crazy pill in this drink, hoping it will get me high so I will sleep with you. I'm no idiot. You can't fool me. You're the biggest jerk I know, and I hope you die out here on this dance floor."
   D: "That's so sweet of you. But I've had all the Diet Coke I need tonight. Thanks, though!"

SCENARIO #2

Chase walks into the frat house prepared to have a little innocent fun. Having transferred to a university from a community college, he isn't used to the "frat scene." Chase is a good kid. He doesn't drink; not because he's morally against it, but because he's underage. However, just because he doesn't get drunk certainly doesn't mean he's backward. Chase is just the opposite; he's outgoing and personable. In fact, back in high school this nineteen-year-old Presbyterian prodigy was known to shake it like a Polaroid picture with the best of them. He even won a "Napoleon Dynamite Dance" competition back at his church. Perhaps known best around church for his good luck with the ladies, Chase's claim to fame is that he is a good dresser. Tonight's no different. Wearing a pair of expensive jeans along with the only Dolce & Gabbana long-sleeved shirt he owns, Chase walks into the frat house looking more like a Calvin Klein model than an ordinary college student. His fashionable shirt is unbuttoned just enough for the ladies to be able to notice that he works out. He talks with a few of his friends. He dances to a couple of his favorite songs. He even "got the party started" with a couple moves so hot the crowd gathered around to cheer him on. But after two hours of dancing, he begins to notice that the mood of the party is changing. Nearly everyone around him has had too much to drink. In fact, a couple of "almost fights" broke out on the dance floor. A couple of girls he knows from his calculus class are passed out on the sofa. In the kitchen, a group of frat guys are having "shot" competitions. Chase begins to feel uncomfortable about his surroundings.

STOP. What would you do if you were Chase? As a Christian, what do you think would be his best response to this situation?

A: Chase should leave right away. He shouldn't have been at the frat party anyway.

B: Chase should stay and try to be a witness to those at the party.

C: Chase should stay. He should preach to those who are sinning and maybe they would repent.

D: Chase should leave quietly and call it an evening.

ANSWERS
SCENARIO #1

A: WRONG ANSWER. Never accept a drink from a stranger. Accept only a drink that has been prepared by a friend.

B: WRONG ANSWER. Never offer a friend a drink from a stranger.

C: CORRECT ANSWER BUT BAD APPROACH. It's good that you turned the drink down, but making harsh accusations is *always* the wrong approach.

D: CORRECT ANSWER. Ding. Ding. Ding. This is the best answer to Sophia's problem. Never accept a drink from a stranger, no matter if it's alcoholic or not, because you never know if the drink has been altered. More than likely, the person handing you a drink is nice, but until you get to know him, get your own drink.

SCENARIO #2

A: GOOD ANSWER. For some Christians in college, going to a party where there is drinking and dancing is not right for them. So if this is your answer you're in good shape!

B: GOOD ANSWER. Some Christians might be very good at being the light of Jesus in this kind of situation.

C: BAD ANSWER. Preaching is probably not the best approach in this situation; I can't imagine drunk partiers are going to be very interested in your soapbox.

D: YET ANOTHER GOOD ANSWER. Depending on how he's feeling, whether he's tempted or not, and whether the situation escalates, a quiet exit could be best.

THE CONCLUDING LIST

The five things from chapter 5 you should have written on your mirror in permanent marker!

1. NEVER WALK ALONE AFTER DARK! For some reason, I just thought of the song, "I wear my sunglasses at night." Do you know that song?

2. WATCH *MY NAME IS EARL* ON NBC. Yeah, so I didn't mention this earlier, but I thought NBC might cover this book on the *Today Show* if I offered them shameless publicity. I'll be waiting for Katie's call.

3. POTATO CHIPS ARE YOUR ENEMY. Well, actually they're your hips, waistline, and butt's enemy. But you'll eventually consider them to be your enemy, too!

4. EXERCISE MAKES YOU MORE ALERT IN CLASSES. It might be good to mention that it also makes your muscles *really* sore. But hey, you look better, right? Isn't that what college is all about? Looking good?

5. TAKE TIME TO CONSIDER YOUR PERSONAL WELLNESS. You (and your mom) will be glad you did.

HEALTH IS A STATE OF COMPLETE
PHYSICAL, MENTAL, AND SOCIAL
WELL-BEING, AND NOT MERELY THE
ABSENCE OF DISEASE OR INFIRMITY.

– WORLD HEALTH ORGANIZATION, 1948

CHAPTER 6

MONEY

(Because you have to learn how to manage the little you have since you just spent it all on college in hopes of making a lot of it in the future)

I'd like to live as a poor man with lots of money.

— PABLO PICASSO

AS A COLLEGE STUDENT, I wasn't very wise with my cash flow. I was pretty much stupid at times. After my first year, I began working part-time jobs to help provide for myself. However, even when I was working at the school's post office or earning a little extra cash through various internships or taking the temporary telemarketing jobs the school would provide, the money didn't last me all that long. I *still* spent every last dime I had on going to the movies, dinners out, CDs that I "had to have," and lending friends cash for their movies, dinners out, and CDs. My extra cash purchases got to be rather ridiculous. Yet let's face it; I couldn't really help spending my college budget of $23 a week. Twenty-three dollars doesn't go too far. And today, that barely covers most people's weekly iTunes needs.

Thank the good Lord that Mom and Dad sent me a little money every once in a while, too. That kept me from having to participate in those weird jobs that some of my college buddies would do to make a little extra money so they could have a Friday night out on the town. One of my friends sold children's books door-to-door. He got so many doors slammed in his face that he lost count. Another friend got fifty dollars a week making "special phone calls" for three hours on a Tuesday evening. Too scared to know what "special phone calls" even meant, I decided not to ask her, and she never offered the information, either. I also had a friend who would sell his plasma (not a type of TV, but a bodily fluid); in fact, he made thirty dollars a visit doing that. By the end of a semester, his forearm looked pretty beat up. It looked like he was a heroin addict. Some of my friends would do just about anything—participate in certain drug testing, sell soft drinks and candy from their dorm rooms, or cut hair—for a few extra bucks.

Crazy enough, one of my *best* friends even called a local hospital to see if they needed any "good-looking, college" sperm donors. He had read somewhere that hospitals offer seventy-five dollars a pop to approved donors. Unfortunately for him, the clinic's nurse told him that if he was under the age of twenty-one—which he was—he would need his parent's signature. Needless to say, when he mentioned it to his mother, and yes, he did *actually mention* it to his mother, she gave him a verbal beating for even considering such a "job." Thankfully, my friend didn't end up fathering any kids.

The need for a little money makes some college students do work that's silly, pointless, humbling, and sometimes, downright inappropriate. But don't despair; the topic of money as it relates to your life at college doesn't have to send you into cardiac arrest *every time* you think about it. You simply need to plan ahead and avoid a few troubled spots. The information provided in this chapter will help you navigate your way through the financial craziness of college, and hopefully, keep you from having to lower yourself to the selling of bodily fluids for a little extra spending money. In fact, let's just pretend I didn't mention that was an option.

A POEM CALLED MONEY!

(Because everyone can use a poem about money)

M *is for the million bucks you'll borrow to get through school*
O *is for the odds and ends you'll buy to make you cool*
N *is for the nasty notes you'll get if you don't pay*
E *is for the extra cash you'll need along the way*
Y *is for the years it takes to pay your Stafford back*
! *is just for emphasis, 'cause a five-lined poem is whack.*

(Now repeat this poem using your best British accent—just do it because it's fun and might annoy your friends.)

THREE VERSES FROM JOB 27 THAT EVERY COLLEGE STUDENT SHOULD KNOW

Even if they make a lot of money
    and are resplendent in the latest fashions,
it's the good who will end up wearing the clothes
    and the decent who will divide up the money.
They build elaborate houses
    that won't survive a single winter. (verses 16-18)

EVERYTHING YOU NEED TO KNOW ABOUT MONEY (THE COLLEGE LIFE PART OF IT, ANYWAY)

BUDGET

(Because God knows you need to know how to spend that twenty-dollar check from Granny!)

College students will usually roll their eyes when you mention their need for a budget at college. You might be rolling your eyes right now. But no matter how many times around your eyes may go, the truth is this: An easy-to-follow budget can help you spend wisely (or should we say, *not* foolishly) and keep you out of financial trouble. Well, except for the financial trouble that comes with a hefty amount of tuition debt. But a budget will help you resist the "buying urges" that often make paying for "after-college life" more difficult.

SIX THINGS YOU NEED TO KNOW AND DO TO CREATE A REASONABLE COLLEGE* LIFE BUDGET

(Because when you're eighteen, you're not inclined to know much about budgeting)

Meet Joe. This little guy is Joe. Joe is going to be helping me explain easy budgeting. In fact, Joe is a real college student. Well, I mean, you're seeing only a silhouette of Joe. So you're not exactly getting the full effect. But trust me; he's a real guy. He will share his budgetary logic with you to help illustrate my points.

UNO.** First and foremost, add up how much money you have to spend each week. Include every source of income that you're expecting. Is your

---

* Even if you're filthy rich, it's imperative to have a financial budget to follow. Also, remember, this budget is for *college life*. Hopefully, you've already figured out a way to pay for your schooling.

** I've used Spanish numbers here because I'm a little tired of looking at one, two, and three. This book has taken me a long time to write, so a simple change like using *uno*, *dos*, and *tres* instead of one, two, and three seems really exciting to me.

mom or dad promising you a weekly allowance? How about Grandma or Grandpa? Aunts? Uncles? Are you a distant cousin to Bill Gates? Whatever your family is graciously giving to you, add it. If you're one of the lucky few who have more scholarship money than the cost of your education, be sure to include that, too. Do you work a part- or full-time job? How much do you bring in on a weekly basis? Once you have a grand total, divide it by the number of weeks you'll be at school.

Joe is choosing not to work his first semester. So his monthly income is a bit limited. His mom and dad are able to give Joe $40 a week toward the simple expenses of college. Joe has allocated $500 a semester from his financial aid package to help him have a little financial freedom. Joe's first semester of school begins on August 21 and ends on December 8. That's a total of sixteen weeks. Sixteen weeks of $40 from Mom and Dad equals $640. When he adds that amount to the $500, he realizes he has $1,140 to spend the first semester. When that amount is divided by sixteen weeks, he finds that his weekly budget is $71.25. Although he's pretty sure that a couple of his relatives will send him a little cash from time to time, he can't bank on that. Therefore, Joe's weekly spending allowance is $71.25.

DOS. Have you checked on the cost of living in your college town? In other words, a trip to the movies in Chestertown, Maryland, is only $6, but a trip to the movies in Manhattan on the Upper West Side is $10.75. That difference of $4.75 is pretty large when you're trying to make a monthly allowance of a couple hundred dollars work for you. Other basic costs to check before you attend include local restaurants, laundry costs, taxi fees, and any other extremity expenses you might find personally useful (like a gym membership, fraternity and sorority dues, and college clubs that might have some costs involved).

Joe is going to school at Vanderbilt University in Nashville, Tennessee. When he researched some of the local costs he found movies to be $8.50, but with his student ID, he can get his movie for $6. Local restaurants were average, too. At most places, if you do not drink alcohol, you can get away with spending somewhere between $8 and $14 for a meal (tip included). One of the most discouraging costs he found in Nashville was its sales tax—9.35 percent. In fact, it ranked highest among major cities in the United States.

FACT:

The Bible teaches us that a portion of our money needs to be given back to the work of God. The Old Testament suggests that this amount should be at least 10 percent of our income. But most theologians suggest today that the 10 percent is simply the beginning. It's pretty obvious throughout Scripture that God loves a happy giver. And you might think it's impossible for you to give your money away to God, mainly because you don't have all that much. But it's not about how much you give; it's more about how you view your money. As Christians, we are called to hold loosely to things of no heavenly value. Although money is needed to live, it should not be our ultimate goal. Generosity should be.

TRES. When developing a college budget, you'll need to know (or make a good estimate of) what costs you will incur. All of your college costs can be put into two categories: fixed costs and changing costs. For some of you, fixed costs include a monthly tuition fee and room and board. If you're paying for these items on a monthly basis, you need to include them in your budget. (If this is the case, hopefully you're making a little more than our friend Joe.) And also, some of you might have car payments, insurance, and parking fees. Fixed costs do not change from month to month. However, your changing costs do. Your inconsistent costs might include entertainment (movies and food), gasoline, toiletries, clothes, car maintenance, books, phone bills (cell and landline), club dues, and/or expenses that might be personal to you.

 **HERE'S JOE'S LIST OF EXPENSES.**

JOE'S FIXED MONTHLY COSTS:

Tuition: $0 (already paid)

Room/board: $0 (already paid)

Car: $0 (1995 Toyota—paid off)

Insurance: $35 (parents pay the rest)

Parking: $20 (divided from the total cost of parking per semester)

Church offering: $15

Total monthly fixed costs: $70

Joe can get his *weekly* cost by dividing $70 by 4 (because approximately four weeks are in one month. You knew that, right?). So . . .

Joe's weekly fixed costs will be: $17.50

JOE'S CHANGING MONTHLY COSTS:

Landline: $0 (already paid)

Cell: $45

Gasoline: $60

Toiletries: $40

Eats: $60

Clothes: $0 (Joe's mom takes care of him)

Movies: $18

Other: $40

Total monthly changing costs: $263

Joe can get his weekly cost by dividing $263 by 4 (because approximately four weeks are in one month. You totally remembered that from before, right?). So . . .

Joe's weekly changing costs will be: $65.75
(FOR YOU ADD PEEPS: Yes, I agree, this is becoming rather boring. But we're almost finished. Why don't you take a break and play fifteen minutes of *Halo* and then come back to this. But *only* fifteen minutes. This is important stuff.)

CUATRO. Okay, so after listing your expenses and figuring out your weekly costs for both fixed and changing expenses, add the amount of your fixed weekly costs to your changing weekly costs. The number you get becomes your total amount for weekly expenses.

 When Joe adds his fixed expenses to his changing expenses, he gets $83.25 as his total weekly expenses.

CINCO. You're almost finished but not *quite*. What you're getting ready to do will be your moment of financial truth. Are you ready? First, let's learn once again from Joe:

Joe felt pretty bad about his budget. Because when he compared his total income to his total expenses, he found that he was planning on spending $12 a week more than he would be making. Luckily for Joe, his granny told him that she would make up the difference by sending him $50 a month. Joe felt pretty good about his budget after his granny told him the good news. "I just wanted to see him do this budget before I gave my money," said Joe's granny. "Budgets are important. Young people need to do them more." Preach it, Granny!

Now your turn. Remember that income total you came up with? Compare that with the number you totaled for your weekly expenses. Here are two potential scenarios:

1. If your expense total is *lower* or equal to your income amount, you're in good shape! Sing praises. Jump up and down. Do a little celebratory jig.

2. However, if your expense amount is *higher* than your income amount, you've got a problem. This pretty much means you're planning on spending more than you'll have on hand. But don't worry; this is why we do a budget, to avoid such situations. You have a few choices*:

- **YOU CAN MAKE, BORROW, OR ASK YOUR PARENTS FOR MORE MONEY.** Just don't sell your blood.

- **YOU CAN CUT SOMETHING FROM YOUR BUDGET.** In other words, you might not be as lucky as Joe, because you have no income from Granny to lean on. In that case, decide that you'll never eat any food outside of the college cafeteria, and then you can simply change the food dollar amount from whatever it is right now to zero. But honestly cutting an entire amount might be difficult. Unfortunately, this applies only to your *changing* costs. Fixed costs can't be changed.

- **YOU CAN ALSO LOWER YOUR *SPENDING* AMOUNT ON SEVERAL ITEMS WITHIN YOUR BUDGET.** Take $10 off of meals, $20 off of clothes, and so on.

ONE LAST THOUGHT ABOUT BUDGETS. Creating a budget gives your parents and you a good chance to talk honestly and openly about money. I highly recommend that you discuss your financial needs with

---

* Just keep in mind that you have to reduce your budget by the difference between your total income and your total expense. If your income is $60 a week and your expenses are $100 a week, you have $40 to diminish out of your budget.

your parents if they're available to you. Do this no matter your parents' financial commitment to you or their financial status. Some parents let their kids earn their own "spending money," and that's fine. Other parents pay for absolutely everything. That has its good and bad points, too. Whatever your situation, talk to someone you trust (parents, guardian, grandparents, or aunt and uncle) about your financial budget. You never know what their insight might be able to do for your situation. You might be planning on spending *way* too much on clothes or CDs. Or you might not have enough planned in other areas. Talking about your planned budget with someone will help you.

And after you've finished listing your income, listing your expenses, and talking with someone, either rewrite your budget neatly or put it into an Excel spreadsheet. And then look at it often! Oh, and a budget doesn't work unless you actually *follow* it.

A FEW WAYS TO HELP YOU FOLLOW YOUR BUDGET

HANG IT UP ON YOUR BATHROOM MIRROR. You can't very well use it if you're not looking at it on a regular basis. If you have a community bathroom, you might just want to hang it in your room somewhere. Of course, be sure that you're not including any personal account information on your printout—just in case your roommate is nosey or has kleptomaniacal tendencies!

PLAN A TIME EACH WEEK TO COMPARE YOUR *SPENDING* WITH YOUR *BUDGET.* This will take you less than fifteen minutes a week, but if your budget is tight it might end up being your lifesaver!

HAVE A FINANCIAL ACCOUNTABILITY PARTNER. If you know that someone is going to be checking in on your spending habits, it might really help you to stay focused on making sure you have enough money to pay your cell phone bill and *not* that video game. Just a thought. More on this later.

BANK ME, BABY!

(A few winning ideas for good, smart banking)

MAKE SURE THE CHECKING ACCOUNT IS FREE. If your college bank is charging you anything for having an account with them, find a new bank. Most banks offer college students free checking accounts.

WHEN USING YOUR BANK CARD, KEEP RECEIPTS. If you're going to keep track of what's in your account and how much you've spent, be sure to keep all of your receipts. However, for even greater tracking, talk to your bank about doing it all online. It's changed my life. No, really, I'm a completely changed man because of my online banking capabilities. You think I'm kidding you. I've changed.

KEEP TRACK OF YOUR ACCOUNT BALANCE. You can do this by going online, visiting an ATM, or calling the bank. Especially if you're not a "checkbook balancer," this is quite necessary to avoid "bouncing check" fees. Some of those fees bounce as high as $40.

ASK MOM AND DAD TO PUT YOUR MONEY IN ELECTRONICALLY. Even if your parents aren't Internet savvy, transferring funds online is easy. Or if they are adamant about *not* using the Internet for banking, tell them to call the bank and transfer the money. This saves on postage *and* time. And it gives you immediate access to the money you so desperately need. In fact, if they are giving you a weekly or monthly allowance for college spending money, tell them to set it up as an automatic transfer.

FOUR SPENDING AREAS THAT GET MANY COLLEGE STUDENTS INTO FINANCIAL HOT WATER
(Yeah, you're gonna love this section)

In 2002, it was estimated that college students combined held more than 200 billion dollars in buying power. That's mucho dinero! Now that you're going to college, you'll be joining the ranks of a very influential group of people. You may never see evidence of this, but the things you like enough to actually purchase greatly influence the products that businesses create. So please, purchase a lot of iPods; I really want that brand to stick around, okay? *Kidding.* But really, some of you get into a lot of trouble with that kind of buying power.

THE SUBJECT: CLOTHING

YOUR FELT NEED TOWARD CLOTHING: Looking good, sexy, and confident.

THE PROBLEM COMES WHEN: You try to live GQ on a Value City budget.

THE FIX: Enact a restraining order between you and the clothing store causing you to fall from grace.

THE REALITY: You do look *really* nice in Prada, but you can't afford it. Target clothes will look almost as good, at about a tenth of the price. And, a note to the women: While your girlfriends may be competitive about who has the trendier, spendier clothing, guys don't care. All they care about is how you *look* in the clothes you wear. You could wear an outfit from Wal-Mart, Target, or Old Navy and they'll never know it as long as the outfit flatters you. So why spend all that money just to impress your catty girlfriends? Case closed.

THE SUBJECT: EATING OUT

YOUR FELT NEED TOWARD EATING OUT: Better (actually edible) food, good fellowship, and a nonfluorescent-lit environment.

THE PROBLEM COMES WHEN: T.G.I. Fridays and P.F. Chang's see you more often than your professors.

THE FIX: Moderation, Moderation, Moderation, Moderation, Moderation, Moderation, Moderation.

THE REALITY: You need the fellowship but gather with your friends in the cafeteria or the student union. The conversation can easily be just as good.

THE SUBJECT: UNDERAGE DRINKING

YOUR FELT NEED TOWARD UNDERAGE DRINKING: I could say that it makes you feel like an adult, but that would probably be giving most of you too much credit. Why don't you just admit it? Most of you do it because someone else did it first and they seemed pretty cool. Except for those of you who drank first and led others astray. Way to go.

THE PROBLEM COMES WHEN: You spend too much money on beer, when you get arrested for underage drinking, and when you vomit all over your best friend's couch. Oh, and let's not forget this one: According to the Bible, being drunk and following God don't go hand in hand. Forgive me if that came across a little judgmental. Sometimes I'm a little over-passionate about certain things—UNDERAGE DRINKING IS ONE OF THEM!

THE FIX: Just don't do it. I promise, you can still be cool without alcohol. Didn't we learn about this in middle school? Some people *never* learn.

THE REALITY: Alcohol is expensive and you're not twenty-one.

THE SUBJECT: ENTERTAINMENT

YOUR FELT NEED TOWARD ENTERTAINMENT: It makes you feel culturally aware. You like to laugh. And you've got a strange crush on Meryl Streep. It's okay; you're young.

THE PROBLEM COMES WHEN: You use your money to see a Drew Barrymore movie instead of paying your overdue Verizon bill.

THE FIX: If possible, pay Verizon and see Drew. But make sure you can do the former before you do the latter.

THE REALITY: Nobody blames you girls for wanting to see a movie where Brad Pitt happens to walk around shirtless half the time. And guys, who would blame you for wanting to see Jessica Alba look amazingly hot in *Fantasti*– actually, *everything*. And nobody's asking, "Why in the world would you want to go see the Dave Matthews Band live?" Well, President Bush or your grandmother might ask you that question. But I won't. Here's the deal; don't spend money on frivolous things unless you have money for frivolous things available in your bank account.

CREDIT CARDS

(Because you don't need one)

The best advice I could offer you about credit cards is to *never* have one of them. Are these harsh words against your little plastic friend? Yes, deservingly so. Credit card debt is bad; it's *real* bad. It's like Scott Stapp bad. No, it's Anna Nicole Smith bad. Let me give it to you in S.A.T. language—credit card debt is to life what Matchbox Twenty is to rock 'n' roll. It's *that* bad. But sadly, despite credit card debt being much worse than any music released by post-1993 Michael Jackson, students are still stupid enough to get into credit card trouble.

I've heard the excuse, "I'm different from other students; I'll pay it every month." Or how about this one? "I'm only using it for school stuff; I don't buy clothes with it." Or, "I might need it for a real emergency." Or don't get me started on this one: "I need to develop credit history." Or this one is my personal favorite: "I get free travel miles on Delta when I use my card." All of those "emergencies and air miles" average out to $2200 worth of credit card debt for card-carrying college graduates. That amount more than doubles for graduate students. So turn the page for my advice.

DON'T GET A CREDIT CARD!!!!

Okay, I promise I'm not a stickler. And I'm not lame. I've just been hired to give you the best advice I can possibly give you about college life. And I'm telling you, from years of experience, I have finally realized that credit card companies do not care about me, they do not want to help me, and I've never used my credit card in a true emergency. I have finally realized that credit card companies are making billions of dollars off my decision to apply for and use their credit card. Their CEOs' kids live like Paris Hilton because of my finance charges. So don't believe the commercials. They don't care about you.

Once you enter college, credit card companies will hound you like the paparazzi. Suddenly everywhere you go, you see advertisements, smiling faces, and commercials all vying for a spot on your eternal credit history. You have to be strong-willed and determined when Lord Visa and Her Majesty the Master Card come into your presence. They will try to manipulate you with T-shirts, clock radios, free air travel, and percentages back. But be strong. Just say no.

GOOD WAYS TO SAY NO TO CREDIT CARD COMPANIES

"NO!" This method is classic, firm, and definitive. What it lacks in depth can be made up in tone. If the credit card companies hound you through the mail, you can most effectively say no by never opening, and immediately throwing away, all credit card applications.

"NO HABLO INGLÉS." This method offers a path toward freedom unless the enemy speaks Spanish.

"I ALREADY HAVE ONE, THANK YOU." This is the only lie I would ever condone.

"NAH, YOU GUYS WANT TO BE PAID BACK. AND THAT TAKES ALL THE FUN OUT OF HAVING ONE." I've actually used this one.

"I DON'T SEE YOU; I AM BLIND." For those of you with no sense of humor, this might seem somewhat mean, but it really works!

"SO SORRY, BUT I AM UNFIT TO BE A KEEPER OF YOUR MONEY." This one allows you to take the blame; it's a good one.

Unfortunately, some of you will not be able to say no. You will fall prey to Lord Visa. Some of you will even fall prey to their younger siblings, Master Gap, Ms. Target, and Brother Sears Card. They will corner you and devour you like bunnies—innocent, sweet little bunnies.

But I know how it is. Sometimes we resist following the best advice—the "DON'T GET A CREDIT CARD" advice. We'd rather prove everyone who ever gave us that brilliant advice wrong. We'd rather show them that *we are different*.

It's a shame you can't resist those credit cards like you resist my good advice. It's the "gold medal" *advice* that is often the most difficult for us to follow. I guess that's the way it is with a lot of things. The best path is often the hardest. Young Frodo learned that in *Lord of the Rings*. Speaking of the Ring, credit card debt is kind of like that ring—powerful, tricky, and dead set on ruining your life.

But, some of you *are* weaklings.

So if you must have a credit card—which if I haven't made this clear, is ridiculous in our days of Visa check cards and multipurpose ATMs—you need to have a few things in place before you credit up.

○ If you must have a credit card, you need to be **DISCIPLINED** in nature. You can't be a weakling. Weaklings get into deep debt. If you're a weakling, it doesn't mean you're a bad person; it just means you have to be extra careful.

○ You must be prepared to pay the **ENTIRE AMOUNT OF THE BILL** each month on its due date. If you can't do this, then you should be prepared to spend lots of time in a personal hell. And I'm betting that's a 1999 Creed concert. This is serious stuff, guys. You do realize that Creed sang "With Arms Wide Open," right? Nobody deserves that kind of torture, especially live.

◦ You must promise to have a **CREDIT CARD ACCOUNTABILITY PARTNER.** Guys have APs to help them stay away from online porn. Girls have APs to keep them on the straight and narrow in relationships. Why shouldn't *you* have an AP for credit cards, too? Chat with someone responsible once a month about how you're handling your credit responsibilities. And for the best results, make your CCAP a parent or an adult friend.

◦ You must swear that you will never purchase anything with a credit card that is not a true necessity. *True* necessity meaning, you actually *need* it, as in, an emergency. And new Pumas are not an emergency. Nor is that Halloween costume you want.

Okay, I'm done talking about credit cards and why you *shouldn't* have one. (DON'T GET ONE!) On with the next section. Wow, that was a workout!

THE SCHOOL JOB
(Because sometimes you need to work)

More than 80 percent of college students are said to have some kind of employment. However, what many don't know is that 39 percent of college students are over the age of twenty-five. This means many students are working and then deciding to go back to school. There's nothing wrong with having a job while you're in school.

In the end, it's your decision. Because of financial situations, many students find it necessary to work. Here are a few things to remember if you're one of the thousands who wake up at 7:00 a.m. for a class and then go to work at noon until 9:00 p.m.

MAKE EDUCATION YOUR PRIORITY. Okay, so you have a job. But don't make your ten to thirty hours a week at Starbucks or Kentucky Fried Chicken your number-one priority. Unless you have a job that is way more important than I'm giving you credit for, make schooling more important than flipping burgers, cleaning toilets, or selling random products.

BE SURE YOUR WORK KNOWS AND RESPECTS YOUR SCHOOL SCHEDULE. There's nothing more frustrating than having a boss who doesn't respect your college lifestyle. When taking a job, be up front about your schedule and the time you'll be able to dedicate to the establishment.

EAT, SLEEP, AND WORK, AND HAVE FUN, TOO. Arrange your schedule in a way that it gives you plenty of time to study, have a social life, *and* get your homework completed.

MAKE SURE YOU PLAN AHEAD. When you work and learn, having a defined schedule becomes even more important. In order for you to keep track of all the places, times, and assignments that need to get done, you will need to be extremely organized.

TELL YOUR EMPLOYER YOUR HOLIDAY SCHEDULE. If you're planning on taking some time off or leaving town during fall, Thanksgiving, Christmas, or spring vacations, let your employer know. By the way, while I'm on the topic, also tell him or her the dates and times of your midterms and finals as soon as they are available.

BE A GOOD EMPLOYEE. If you do a bad job and get your employer upset with you, you're going to be adding unneeded stress to your life. As a college student, you don't need any more stress than what is already put on you. And, you'll like your job more if you work hard and do a good job.

TWO ADDICTIONS PREVALENT IN COLLEGES
That Cause Great Financial Problems (for Guys More Than Girls)

1. ONLINE GAMBLING. Many college students, especially guys, have taken to the card game craze like flies to poop. One of the major ways students are passing time these days is through online gambling. With a credit card and inexperienced carding skills, these young men are racking up huge amounts of debt and paying the price by having to forfeit their educations. "Gambling addiction is four to five times more common among youth and college students than among the adult population," says Christine Reilly, executive director of the Institute for Research on Pathological Gambling at Harvard Medical School's Division on Addiction.

2. PORNOGRAPHY. Like gambling, pornography is also an addiction that can soak you financially dry. Whether it's online movies, websites, sex shops, strip clubs, or 1-900 numbers, for someone with even a small problem, bank accounts can be drained and credit cards maxed out on this kind of addiction. If you're one of the thousands who spend a great deal of time and money surfing the Internet looking at pornography, please find help. Visit XXXChurch.com and/or find a counselor in your area who specializes in sexual addictions.

A SUPER-COOL POEM ABOUT THE FIVE TYPES OF MONEY-WASTING STUDENTS

5. THE "FLASHY" STUDENT

These types of students sure get their kicks
by wearing Gucci and boasting fashionable picks.
With cash in their pockets and credit card glee,
they make you feel lame for wearing Old Navy jeans.

4. THE "EVERY NIGHT" STUDENT

When this friend's around, she's asking again,
"You wanna go out? I've got money to spend."
As she's spending hers, you're spending yours, too.
But when it's all said and done, you both look like a fool.

3. THE "NO MONEY" STUDENT

When you're hangin' with this student, they eventually shout,
"DO YOU GOT A FIVE I CAN BORROW?
GOSH, I'M ALL OUT!"
They'll borrow and promise to pay you back quick.
But don't fall for their lies; it's all part of their shtick.

2. THE "PRETEND RICH" STUDENT

This student's talk finds a whole lot of ears.
They speak of riches galore to all of their peers.
But when the truth is found out and we hear 'bout their net,
It's more likely than not they're in serious debt.

1. THE "IN-LOVE" STUDENT

Don't fall for the person who loves you for this:
the things that you buy them. You'll only get dissed.
When they've taken your pennies,
your innocence, your world,
Watch out my dear brothers, this one's usually a girl.

THINK THE COST OF COLLEGE ISN'T WORTH IT?

You might want to think again. According to a recent study, over a working lifetime, the typical college graduate earns roughly 75 percent more than a high-school grad does.

THE CONCLUDING LIST

The five things from chapter 6 that you should have put onto a microchip and inserted on the left side of your neck.

1. DON'T GET A CREDIT CARD! You hate me now, I know.

2. STAY AWAY FROM PORNOGRAPHY. It costs you more than just your innocence. If it becomes a struggle, get help.

3. SHOP AT OLD NAVY, WAL-MART, AND TARGET. You don't need designer ANYTHING.

4. MAKE A BUDGET, THEN FOLLOW IT. This will save you from having to make the dreaded phone call to Mom and Dad to say, "I need more money!" They'd much rather you call and say, "I'm just calling to say hi and that I love you!"

5. TITHE. The less money you waste the more you have to spend on being generous to the things that truly matter.

THERE IS NO DUTY WE SO MUCH

UNDERRATE AS THE DUTY

OF BEING HAPPY.

— ROBERT LOUIS STEVENSON

CHAPTER 7

INVOLVEMENT AND FUN

(You can have a lot of fun at college, but only if you're involved)

Man consists of two parts, his mind and his body, only the body has more fun.
— WOODY ALLEN

COLLEGE INVOLVEMENT WAS A bit overwhelming and awkward for me in the beginning. It's that way for a lot of students. Having grown up in a small private school in rural America, I tended to be shy and not all that quick to involve myself in too many things. Taking my first two years at a community college didn't help that cause, either. But when I went to Belmont, I realized that if I was going to survive and thrive away from the familiarity of my family and friends, I was going to have to get involved.

At first, involvement was pretty hard. It will be difficult for many of you. For others, it will come as natural as breathing. For every student I knew who would jump into groups, into clubs, or on to teams at the drop of a hat, there was another student who had to work a little bit harder to feel any level of comfort getting involved.

I wanted to be involved, but it was simply hard for me to muster up enough courage. But upon seeing how involvement impacted other students, I slowly developed the courage to move forward into experiences that weren't necessarily comfortable, but they were necessary for my personal growth.

Being involved opened a whole new world of opportunity and experiences.

For me, it was through involvement that I gained my closest and dearest friendships, met the girl who became my first serious girlfriend, and ended up finding a few personal passions, a supportive community, and some emotional and spiritual stability. Whether it was a small Bible study or the Music Business society or the theology book discussion group or getting involved in the production of concerts, the volunteering for community projects or playing pool in a tournament with seven friends, involvement changed my life. *Why?* Because it allowed me the opportunity to relate to new people, an environment to grow, and the lesson of giving. I'm pretty sure I wouldn't be doing what I do now if I had resisted getting involved.

When you're involved, it makes *all* the difference in college. So as you consider your first semester, make sure you plan "involvement and fun" into your schedule. This chapter will get you started.

Getting involved on campus is the best way for you to have a full, vivacious college experience. I love the word *vivacious*. There's just something quite gripping about the word. It's one of those words that actually *sounds* sinful—yet it's not at all. It's kind of like the word *secretion*, or *immaculate* or *fluke*. Go ahead; try saying *vivacious* slowly. Sounds sinful, doesn't it?

Okay, back to the *actual* book content.

College is made *vivacious* because of the diverse opportunities you have to interact with other people, grow as an individual, and even make an impact on the lives of people, your community, and sometimes the world. If you attend a big school, getting involved will help make your campus seem smaller. If you go to a smaller school, involvement often brings entire campuses together around a cause, rally, or idea.

And for you (like it did for me), involvement will help you connect with the experience of college. It will help you become comfortable in your new surroundings, and it will give you purpose. Fun and involvement define your experience, not just in college, but also in life.

FIVE REASONS TO GET INVOLVED IN COLLEGE

1. Involvement gives you an on-campus voice.

2. Involvement lets you learn about yourself.

3. Involvement shows you your personal strengths *and* weaknesses.

4. Involvement gives you skills and experience.

5. Involvement is a great way to develop new interests.

ONE VERSE FROM ECCLESIASTES 8 THAT EVERY COLLEGE STUDENT SHOULD KNOW

So, I'm all for just going ahead and having a good time—the best possible. The only earthly good men and women can look forward to is to eat and drink well and have a good time—compensation for the struggle for survival these few years God gives us on earth. (verse 15)

EVERYTHING YOU NEED TO KNOW ABOUT BEING INVOLVED IN COLLEGE . . .
(Because every one of you needs to be involved in something)

- -

CLUBS, SOCIETIES, AND GROUPS
(Because the biggest problem you'll have is in choosing what not to do)

STUDENT GOVERNMENT
Did you fail to become class president in high school? Did you lose by two votes to the ditsy, hot blonde girl in your English class? It's okay; college will bring you a new chance to serve your student body through student government. Why not run for class president of your freshman class? The world is your oyster—so find your pearl!

Similar to student council in many high schools, your college's student government works to advocate change for students. And in most colleges, it also becomes very much like a sounding board for students' concerns. Just remember, student government varies by school, but like most clubs or societies, SGs have regular meetings and they offer a variety of ways for students to be involved. Even if you don't want to run for president or VP, most student governments also have weekly meetings you can go to and volunteer opportunities within the campaigns. They also offer a great avenue for connecting with influential people on the campus and in the community. Oh, and don't forget this one: Some student governments also offer internships. For more information on student government, check your school's website or contact the student life office.

GREEK LIFE
Living the life of a frat guy or a sorority girl varies widely depending on the school and organization. It wasn't too long ago that students joined the "Greeks" because they offered, managed, and organized all the *fun* and *excitement* a college campus offered. But over the years, most schools began looking for their own ways to improve the quality

of campus life. So for most college students, Greek life doesn't play as much of a significant role as it did twenty or thirty years ago. And in fact, because of bad press and a few high-profile violent acts committed at frat houses, memberships of fraternities and sororities have declined.

Sadly, today, F (fraternity) and S (sorority) houses are often best known for their parties, wild fun, and free-flowing beer. But those are certainly not the only "benefits" (as some call it) to Greek life. Greeks are also known for helping students develop leadership skills, providing networking opportunities, and offering a good place to develop college companionship. Any of these would be good reasons to look into being involved in an F or S while at college. Greek life also offers a few substantial volunteering opportunities.

Also, it's good to remember that a few colleges offer Christian frats and sororities. However, regardless of the type of F or S, you want to find out as much information about the group as you can *before* you join. Greek life can be rewarding, but it can also be a lot more stress than it's worth.

BEFORE YOU JOIN OR PLEDGE, FIND OUT THIS INFORMATION

- Know the history of the F or S. When did it begin? What's their primary focus?
- Is the organization at more than one college? What reputation does it have at the school you're attending?
- What are your school's rules on hazing? Can you find any history of violent acts against pledges?
- Talk to someone who was/is involved. How did he or she benefit from being involved? Any problems?
- Are parties the F's or S's only strength or simply an added bonus? Do the parties ever get too wild?
- Do they allow underage drinking?
- Find out the F's or S's "law-abiding" history.
- How much are the dues?
- As a Christian, you will also want to check out the organization's moral standing on campus.

Once you know the information, you can make your own assessment about whether or not your college life should be spent living Greek.

OTHER CLUBS

Some large universities offer literally hundreds of clubs and/or organizations. And even what some smaller colleges have to offer can be quite extensive. It's important to do the research ahead of time. When you know what a college offers, it will help you decide early about how and with whom to be involved. Most colleges, even the smallest of community colleges, have groups that meet for a varied number of reasons. Most often, the following topics and/or causes are the most popular.

ELEVEN OF THE MOST POPULAR REASONS COLLEGE STUDENTS COME TOGETHER ON A REGULAR BASIS (IN NO PARTICULAR ORDER)

1. Faith or religion (Campus Crusade, Navigators, and so on)

2. Sexual orientation (LGBT—Lesbian, Gay, Bisexuals, and Transgender—clubs)

3. Political standing or belief (everything from the death penalty to both sides of the abortion issue)

4. Talent or hobby (various clubs celebrating scrapbooking to trumpet playing)

5. Educational (Latin, math, and science clubs tend to be popular)

6. Lifestyle (clubs that celebrate being everything from vegetarian to abstinent)

7. Social justice (AIDS in Africa, famine, and poverty often spark clubs at colleges)

8. Theater (if you like acting or are an acting major)

9. Local interests (in Wisconsin, it might be agriculture; in California, it might be surfing)

10. Culture (clubs that celebrate things like good wine, art, and music)

11. Sports (from intramural to the big ten, sports make people happy and cause them to gather in large groups)

Check with your college for more information about what is offered, and then get involved!

HOW TO FIND THE CLUB OR SOCIETY THAT'S RIGHT FOR YOU

- WHAT ARE YOUR INTERESTS? During the first week of school, when every campus group is boasting their existence (and they will be), be sure to look for groups and/or gatherings that share your interests. Whether it's a sport or cause or belief, your basic interests offer a good outlet for you to find a common group of friends at college.

- WHAT ARE YOUR NEEDS? In search of spiritual well-being? Do you need extra assistance in a particular area of science? Many colleges offer clubs and societies designed to help you find some direction in specific areas of your life.

- WHAT ARE YOUR GIFTS? Some schools have huge chess clubs. Others have clarinet societies or swimming clubs. If you have a particular gifting, it might be a good way to involve yourself in your college experience.

EXTRA CREDIT: REMEMBER TO ALSO CONSIDER THE FOLLOWING BEFORE YOU GET INVOLVED IN A CLUB OR SOCIETY:

- **COST.** Is there an ongoing fee associated with the group? Does it fit within your budget?
- **TIME.** How much time would you have to dedicate to the group?
- **SCHEDULE.** Will this group be meeting at a time that is good for you?
- **SIZE.** Is the group too big or too small for you?
- **SANCTIONED.** Is the club sanctioned by the college? If not, be a little careful.
- **CONTENT.** Is the club focused on positive and growth-oriented subjects? Does the club help you grow as a student or does it promise to turn you into a lush? Of course, your club doesn't have to be Christian in nature, but you should make sure you're joining something that won't force you to compromise your personal values.

CLUBS/ACTIVITIES WITHIN YOUR MAJOR

If you are like most freshmen, you probably aren't ready to declare a major yet. In fact, you may not even know if you want to go for a BA (Bachelor of Arts) or a BS (Bachelor of Science)! Once you have your options narrowed down, partaking in an activity within your major is a great way to meet people who have a like interest in that particular area of study. For instance, if you think you may be interested in majoring in public relations, check out the marketing or journalism department's Public Relations Society of America meetings. By attending one, you will probably meet at least one professor from the department, as well as many students. You will also be exposed to a closer look at the subject of public relations. Virtually ever major has some sort of organization affiliated with it. Check out the department's website or speak with your advisor if you are interested in partaking in a specific club.

THREE COLLEGE STUDENTS TALK ABOUT GETTING INVOLVED

I got involved with Campus Crusade for Christ during my first semester. The weekly meetings helped me remain focused on my faith throughout my college experience. They also gave me an amazing atmosphere in which to make friends. Some of the guys and girls I met that first semester at Crusade are some of my best friends today.

−JAMI, 25, ALUM OF GEORGE MASON UNIVERSITY

Playing intramural rugby was the best thing that ever happened to me in college. It not only allowed me an outlet to exercise and gain confidence, it also brought me a lot of good opportunities to talk with my friends about faith, life, and stuff like that. I loved those guys. Heck, I still love those guys. And a couple of them are following Jesus now because I took a chance on a sport that I knew nothing about.

−WILL, 28, ALUM OF OHIO STATE

I was pretty good on the debate team in high school, so I used that as a way for me to get involved in college, too. It gave me a lot of confidence and also allowed me the opportunity to meet some amazing people, not only from my school, but from colleges all across the country. I met my wife through the debate team. We debated against each other. My school won!

−DANIEL, 26, ALUM OF UNIVERSITY OF GEORGIA

ACTIVE WAYS TO BE INVOLVED

('Cause why not get your exercise and be involved at the same time?)

- -

INTRAMURAL SPORTS

Even if you were an athletic superstar in high school, it's a lot more difficult to become a collegiate athletic superstar. That's where intramurals come in. Intramurals are the perfect way for you to hone your athletic talents, while not having the pressures of performance and practice of collegiate sports.

This might surprise you, but intramural sports are very popular on many college campuses. And actually, intramurals are highly competitive. So do not hesitate to get your best game face on and take it out on the "amateur" playing field. Whether it's rugby, basketball, wrestling, or volleyball, playing your favorite sport against the regular guys and girls at your college can be quite exhilarating. I highly recommend it.

So check out your school's gym for information, or talk with your RA. Usually the types of sports will vary by season. Unless you enjoy playing Ultimate Frisbee in eight inches of snow.

PRACTICAL ADVICE ABOUT FUN AND INVOLVEMENT

If you don't know what Ultimate Frisbee is, you may be in trouble on many campuses. College students have become notorious for playing this fun, fast-paced sport. Sure, Ultimate Frisbee is noncontact. And some believe it's a rather strange sport considering that it's a combination of soccer, basketball, football, and netball. The rules are simple enough for anyone who wants to pick it up. Even those who don't consider themselves athletic can join in the fun. Find out more at WhatIsUltimate.com.

BE A SPORTY SPECTATOR

So maybe you're *not* good enough to play intramurals or perhaps you simply don't have the time. So why don't you support those who *are* good enough and *have* enough time by becoming a regular spectator at your school's sporting events? Okay, not every school has a basketball team like Duke University (Go Blue Devils!) or a football team like Florida State, but that doesn't mean you can't enjoy a little collegiate competition now and then. No matter what school you go to, it might be fun to actually get involved in the local sporting scene.

Just because your college's team is a second-to-last place basketball squad in Division III doesn't mean the games aren't entertaining. So give it a shot. Even if you're one of those artsy students who find sports to be the biggest waste of time, you might be surprised at how much fun you'll experience when you feel an energy-packed crowd of screaming, raging fans of college football or basketball. Just ask any football fan at a school like Virginia Tech or UW Madison; they'll tell you how much *fun* it can be. Heck, at schools like these, even the marching bands are considered cool.

FIVE RULES FOR BEING A GOOD SPECTATOR

- **WEAR YOUR SCHOOL COLORS**. Don't go to a game unprepared. Proudly declare your faithful collegiate heart by wearing your affections on your back. Many students actually wear their spirit everywhere they can imagine—pants, hat, gloves, underwear, and socks!
- **DON'T EVER WEAR THE *OTHER* TEAM'S COLORS**. Some freshmen accidentally wear the opposing team's colors. You're apt to get booed right out of your seat. So be careful. Sports fans are

serious and can be rather obnoxious.

- WHEN EVERYBODY ELSE IS DOING SOMETHING, YOU SHOULD DO IT, TOO. Whether it's a silly cheer or a dumb dance or screaming crazy slogans at the other team, don't ask why; just join in. Unless it's illegal—then I don't recommend doing it.
- DON'T CRY OVER A LITTLE SPILLED BEER. People around you are apt to be drinking. If you happen to get splashed with a little of Milwaukee's best, don't complain. Just laugh it off. If you don't, you'll be seen as a party pooper, and you don't want to be that!
- WATCH THE CHEERLEADERS IF YOU DON'T KNOW WHAT'S GOING ON. When they're screaming or jumping up and down or looking rather anxious, then be all of those things, too!

THEATER

A great way to meet people and learn something new is by being in a school-produced play or musical. Who cares if you have *no* desire to be as famous as the very talented Anthony Hopkins (or *untalented* as any of the actors on *The O.C.*)? Acting, singing, or helping with the lighting is still a great way to be involved. You don't have to be an acting major or music major to do this. In fact, many schools (not all) offer students from any major the chance to participate in certain campus plays, shows, and musicals. If you love acting or singing, you might be surprised by how much fun you have on stage. For those of you with no acting talent, why not try your hand at being a stage*hand*? Many students join the college theater and find talent they never knew existed. However, before you get your hopes up, check with the drama department for more detail.

YOGA, WEIGHT LIFTING, AND BASKETBALL— GETTING INVOLVED AT THE GYM

A large percentage of colleges have at least one gym where students are allowed to work out. Many of these gyms offer a variety of classes including swimming, yoga, weight lifting, and basketball, just to name a few. For some students who are just getting acclimated to their schedule, working out can be difficult to fit in (just like I mentioned in chapter 5). Yet, if a class is offered at a set time, some find that they are more likely to attend. Fitness classes are also a great way to build a new friendship by attending with a buddy or meeting new people. Use your desire to *bend* it like Madonna to your advantage: Do Pilates and make new friends.

OUTDOOR ACTIVITIES

Though geography (and frankly, your overall coordination) dictates the types of activities you'll be able to pursue, in broad terms, you can't ignore that the outdoors plays a big role in a student's campus experience. Some of the types of outdoor activities offered at your school may include:

○ Running
○ Kayaking
○ Sailing
○ Skiing
○ Surfing
○ Climbing
○ Horseback riding
○ Scuba diving
○ Biking
○ Hiking
○ Frolicking

One benefit to getting involved in outdoor activities such as these is simply the opportunity to try something new. Often, campus outdoor groups will have all the supplies you need to participate, and the fees are more modest than they would be if you went on your own. Plus, you meet other students who have a similar interest. Many outdoor activities are also great for health. Exercise doesn't hurt any of us.

DO SOMETHING GOOD: VOLUNTEER

No matter what other commitments you have (school, work, church, athletics), you should make an effort to volunteer at least a few hours each month. Did you know that college graduates are more than one and one-half times more likely to volunteer than those who didn't graduate from college? That's a very good thing. Oftentimes, those who volunteer are not only benefiting someone else, but they are benefiting themselves, too.

One of the great facets of volunteering is that whatever you have an interest in, a need for your help or time or money probably exists. So if you have a passion for children, you could volunteer to be a tutor or a mentor. If you like gardening, you could volunteer at a developing neighborhood or at a community park.

Your school may have a volunteer office where you can go to learn about local volunteer opportunities. Sometimes, these offices will also offer "alternative breaks," which are trips offered during school breaks that involve volunteering—such as a Habitat for Humanity trip or a church-related mission trip. Also, a local church or shelter might be able to assist you in finding valuable volunteer opportunities.

PLACES TO VOLUNTEER

More than 600,000 charities and nonprofit organizations exist nationwide. Some of the following large organizations might be a good place to start when looking for a way to volunteer in your college community.

- Red Cross
- Boys and Girls Club
- YMCA
- Habitat for Humanity
- Boy Scouts of America
- Girl Scouts of America
- Salvation Army
- Big Brothers, Big Sisters

∘ World Vision
∘ The ONE Campaign

You can visit GuideStar.org and research nonprofits in your community. Or do a Google search on any of the above organizations. Each organization has different requirements for volunteering.

YOU BENEFIT MOST WHEN YOU VOLUNTEER BECAUSE . . .

∘ You're not thinking about your needs; you're actually being unselfish.
∘ You're given the chance to see and experience someone else's reality.
∘ You're not getting any financial reward in return.
∘ You're living out Jesus' command to be a light in your community.

SPIRITUAL INVOLVEMENT

Christian groups offer us amazing opportunities to worship, connect, and make a difference on our campus.

CAMPUS MINISTRY

Like I've mentioned before, the college experience is a time where many students' faith in Christ is developed, challenged, and intensified. No matter if you attend a small Christian university where most people think alike or if you go to a larger school where many belief systems exist, becoming involved in a campus ministry that meets on a regular basis will help you in your desire to connect and grow spiritually. That's important on any campus. Your spiritual life is the most important facet of your being because it affects every other aspect of your life. Growing and nurturing that part of your life will help you remain grounded in the other parts of your life. Although joining a campus ministry will not solve *all of your* spiritual needs, it is a great place to start.

Campus ministries give you the opportunity to meet people with similar values and faith. Usually, these organizations have trained leaders whose main goal is to empower you to look to God for life and fulfillment. Also, most campus ministries offer both small-group activities (Bible studies, praise and worship team involvement, and volunteer opportunities) and large-group activities (retreats, mission trips, and large gatherings like concerts and seminars). A few of the most well-recognized campus faith-based organizations include:

- Campus Crusade for Christ
- InterVarsity Christian Fellowship (IV)
- Alpha Omega
- Navigators
- Youth for Christ
- Youth With A Mission
- Chi Alpha Christian Ministries
- Baptist Student Union
- Fellowship of Christian Athletes
- Reformed University Fellowship

If you come from a particular Christian denomination, you may also find a campus ministry that's designed specifically for you. Most ministries will be well advertised around campus during your first couple weeks of activities. So keep your eyes peeled for any signs with fishes, crosses, or pics of Jesus. (In other words, if you see any kind of cheesy Christian clipart, read the poster. You're probably very close to finding a Christian ministry or, eerily, something *not* Christian at all.* So read the poster or ad carefully.)

Make sure you learn about the different ways you can get involved with organizations like those mentioned as soon as you get to school. The people already involved are excited to meet freshmen (fresh blood!)

---

* Some campus ministries are not well known. If your college has a ministry that you've *never* heard about, just make sure you do some research on them before you attend. You don't want to involve yourself into anything "cult-like."

and help them get acclimated to campus life. More important, they want to invest in you spiritually. So whether it is going on a weekend retreat, getting involved in a small-group Bible study, or greeting at the weekly meetings, don't be afraid to jump in. You will definitely be glad you did—from both a spiritual perspective and a social perspective. (Hey, you might find a great boy or girl to try your best dating skills on. After at least a semester of friendship, of course. Nobody wants to miss that opportunity.) When you're an upperclassman, you'll be able to remember when you first walked into your ministry, not knowing anyone.

SMALL TALK WITH UNIVERSITY PASTOR DAVE HUNT

Dave Hunt was also a student at Belmont when I was there. Today, he's a worship pastor at a local church and also the Campus Minister at Belmont. Knowing that he sees ministry at work on campus every day, I thought it would be good to get his perspective on ministry involvement. Here's an excerpt from that interview:

MATTHEW: Dave, why do you believe it is important for college freshmen to get connected to a faith-based community while at college?

DAVE: College is such an incredible time of growth for individuals. Having a faith-based community allows people to be able to explore what they believe and why. So many people who grow up in church come to college and find that they have believed in Jesus because their parents did, or because they were supposed to. It's in the college years, many times, that ideas and beliefs about faith and God are hashed out, tested, discovered, or awakened. This can happen in an individual's life on his or her own, but it is so great to not have to walk that path alone.

MATTHEW: Are there any specific elements you think a student should look for in a group or ministry before taking part?

DAVE: In my experience in campus ministry, I have seen students time and again try to connect with several different groups at the beginning of the fall semester, yet they end up staying with the group where they find people that are like-minded. It's been interesting to see students who grew up in a Methodist church connect in a Baptist Campus Ministry or someone who grew up in a Lutheran church connect at Reformed University Fellowship. The same could be said for almost all the denominations represented on campus because students want to find people who are like-minded.

MATTHEW: What are the greatest challenges a student faces when trying to become engaged in Christian community?

DAVE: One of the greatest challenges is the reality that college students are often inconsistent. There are so many things pulling at the attention of students that they are easily swayed to go to this event or that and not be consistently involved in a Christian community. One of the aspects of community that allows people to trust and walk deeply is consistency. If students are consistent in their involvement, they will be more apt to experience the benefits more consistently, too.

MATTHEW: Any other hints that might help college students stay focused on their faith while at college?

DAVE: I would encourage students to discover what they believe and why they believe it and to be open to hearing other views. Our God is beyond our comprehension and I am amazed at how vast He is. The older I get, the more I learn about God. However, whenever I learn something new about His character, it's as though He's opened a door into another world. I'm continually amazed by the mercy and grace of our God and that He would choose to be involved in our lives. We must never lose the wonder and sense of mystery as we pursue our Maker.

A FEW MORE COMMENTS ABOUT INVOLVEMENT AND CAMPUS MINISTRIES

- ○ **CHRISTIAN GROUPS ARE SOMETIMES CLIQUISH.** Do not let that stop you from getting involved. If it's necessary, go and talk to your leader about helping you get started. And when you finally do become a part of the ministry, remember how you felt when you first began. Then, treat the next freshmen according to how Christ would desire you to.
- ○ **DON'T GO ONE TIME AND NEVER GO AGAIN.** Before you proclaim a particular ministry boring or stupid, make sure you give it a chance first. Attend its meetings at least three or four times before you make a decision to not go again. Also, if you do quit one, make sure you try another group.
- ○ **GO WITH AN OPEN MIND AND HEART.** You don't know how God may use this new group of people to affect your spiritual life. Let your eyes be opened and your heart moved when He deems it necessary.

A PERSONAL PERSPECTIVE ABOUT GETTING INVOLVED IN CHRISTIAN MINISTRY

By Mandy Leigh Runnels, 23
Florida State University/BA—Fall 2000
George Washington University/MA—Spring 2003

Attending FSU was a dream come true for me. As an avid football fan, it was the perfect fit for my interests and social calendar, but not for my growth in faith. Raised as a Southern Baptist, I had the church and its teachings running through my veins. But once I was out on my own and did not have to report to church three to four times a week, I chose what seemed to be a liberating path. I chose wrong.

After three years of focusing on nothing but building my social clientele, I watched a very wise young lady in my sorority step out in faith and start a "Greek" Bible study. Greek BASIC (Brothers and Sisters in Christ) primarily targeted members of the Greek community on Florida State's campus. It was a weekly praise and worship group that started small, but soon became an outlet for Christians on campus who never before had an opportunity and forum to share their faith with other students.

This was a tough step for me to take. It meant breaking away from the constant party that was my life. Although I did not completely sever my ties with the party crowd, for the first time in three years I really felt God's hand. The issue wasn't that He stopped talking to me; it was that I stopped listening to Him.

Greek BASIC was the turning point in my life. When asked if I would have led my life differently back then, the answer would be "no." God let me run my life the way I thought it should be run, because He knew that I needed to hit rock bottom to realize the amazing gift He had given me. Because of His grace, I am able to share my faith as a Christian woman who has seen the struggles of a young Christian girl afraid to make that step.

My advice to Christians who are about to embark on the college journey — always remember that no matter where you are, what you do, and what decisions you make, you are always covered by God's amazing grace. The one true constant you can always depend on is Jesus. You are never out of His reach and never too far gone for Him. And so don't be afraid to make a bold step in faith when God asks you to. More than likely, someone is watching you. Your actions might just change his or her life. They changed mine.

EDUCATIONAL INVOLVEMENT
(Surprisingly, some people can't get enough of learning. And I guess that's a good thing.)

- -

LECTURES

Yes, you will attend hours of academic lectures every week, so why would I put lectures in with involvement? Occasionally your school or a campus organization will host a lecture by respected professors, well-known political personalities, or famous entertainers. In spite of those classroom lectures, you might find many of these distinguished lecturers very interesting and informative. Although you might disagree with the point of view, it will give you an opportunity to hear and participate in the discussions that happen afterward. If you aren't there, you can't have an opinion. It was during these situations that I personally learned a great deal about what I believed to be true about the world. God used people of all walks of life to challenge me to rely more heavily upon the truth I found in Scripture.

EXTRA CREDIT: Chances are, while you are in college, a major presidential election will take place. Undoubtedly, lectures and debates will be scheduled during this season. People on both sides of the political aisle will be asked to speak about the issues, the candidates, and their ideas about the future of our country. These types of lectures are well worth attending because they will probably broaden your view and educate you about ideas with which you weren't previously familiar. Furthermore, the speaker may in fact strengthen one of your viewpoints, enabling you to talk about your opinions and thoughts in a more educated manner.

STUDY ABROAD

For those of you who elect to do so, studying abroad is often one of the most rewarding parts of a student's college experience. This might surprise you, but many universities have relationships with colleges all over the world. And you might also be shocked by how affordable it can be for you to spend one of your semesters learning about marine biology in New Zealand or psychology in Norway or art history in Spain. Your campus probably has a study abroad office (most do) where you can spend hours researching the variety of locations around the world. By studying abroad through your school, you will be able to take classes with credits that will transfer back to the States. So traveling abroad does not necessarily mean that you will have to go to school for an extra semester. Be sure to chat with your advisor for more information. Or go to StudyAbroad.com and get the four-one-one about this once-in-a-lifetime opportunity.

FUN ISN'T AN EXTRACURRICULAR ACTIVITY; YOU NEED IT

Remember your days in middle school when your teacher would let you go outside only if your schoolwork was finished or if it was a particularly warm, sunny day? Gone were the days of planned recess. That was a sad day, huh? That, and the day they stopped letting us take naps after lunchtime. I've learned over the years that *fun* should never be an extracurricular activity; it should always be a part of what you're doing.

Before college, fun is easy. But as you get older, beginning when you go to college, fun (the good, moral kind) gets left out of life's equation. In fact, it's often the very first thing we omit from our schedules when life gets busy or complicated or overwhelming. Sure, you'll pursue having fun for the first few weeks of college. But eventually, you'll get to a point in your semester where you're *so* busy with classes, research papers, and finals that you forget about *your* emotional, physical, mental, *and* spiritual need for fun. I'm not so sure that removing the *one fun thing* out of your schedule is a good move. Now, some of you will have your schedules so chock-full of *fun* activities that you won't have time for work. (And that's not going to be good for you either.)

As you enter this new stage of life, remember that having fun is just as important as your classes, journaling times, Bible studies, alone times, study times, and so on. In fact, the benefits that your brain receives when you choose to have fun are often *much* more stimulating than other activities. Also, many believe that someone who has regularly scheduled fun actually performs better in other areas of life. This means you might have to plan ahead for fun. You might actually have to schedule it in. When you get settled in your new life at school, make a point to look at the calendar and mark down times and dates where a little unadulterated fun can happen. Resist the temptation to make *fun* the first item you remove from your life when your life gets tough. You need the fun. You'll be happier keeping the fun.

A SONG (HAVE SOME FUN)

When you find your roommate using your bar of soap
(have some fun)
When your only friend is studying to be Pope
(have some fun)
When your professor proclaims "you're gonna fail my class"
If your poor little butt breaks out in a rash
When you make the mistake of being a wee-bit crass (have some fun)

When you live too far to go home for Thanksgiving
(have some fun)
When your roommate can't miss "Martha Stewart's Living"
(have some fun)
When your parents come visit the week before finals
When your date shows up wearing black and blue vinyl

When you're taking a class that's about all things vaginal
(have some fun)

When the dorm gets locked with you not inside
(have some fun)
When two papers are due with a lab on the side
(have some fun)
When it's Friday night and you have two bucks to spend
And you're home watching TiVo without all your friends
When your four years are up and they declare this the end
(have some fun)

SOME GOOD QUOTES ABOUT HAVING FUN

Fun does not come in sizes.
> —BART SIMPSON, WISE, SARCASTIC CARTOON CHARACTER

The true object of all human life is play. Earth is a task garden; heaven is a playground.
> —G. K. CHESTERTON, A THINKER WHO WAS MUCH SMARTER THAN MOST OF US

The human race has only one effective weapon—and that is laughter.
> —MARK TWAIN, A GUY WHO WROTE LOTS OF BOOKS, BUT NOT THIS ONE

THE CONCLUDING LIST

Write these five things from chapter 7 on a sheet of paper and put that sheet of paper in a container and bury it in the ground. On the day you graduate, dig it up and dance around like you've found something you've been looking for for years! Or claim it's from 1824! You might get written up in the local newspaper!

1. KNOW GREEK BEFORE YOU GO GREEK! Frats and sororities are fun, but they can also be damaging, so do the research.

2. VOLUNTEER. Do some good for someone else. You might find it's actually fun.

3. YOU NEED FUN! Believe it or not, having fun makes you a better student.

4. GO ON A SHORT-TERM MISSION PROJECT. This is a great way to connect with other Christians and make the world a better place.

5. READ THIS BOOK FIVE TIMES AND GET ALL OF YOUR FRIENDS TO BUY IT. Now, that's fun! Well, it is for me.

"THE PERSON WHO TRUSTS ME WILL NOT
ONLY DO WHAT I'M DOING BUT EVEN
GREATER THINGS, BECAUSE I, ON MY
WAY TO THE FATHER, AM GIVING YOU
THE SAME WORK TO DO THAT I'VE BEEN
DOING. YOU CAN COUNT ON IT."

— JESUS (JOHN 14:12)

CHAPTER 8

MISCELLANEOUS

(All the stuff that didn't fit anywhere else in the book!)

Don't agonize. Organize.
— FLORYNCE KENNEDY

HAVING COVERED EVERYTHING FROM relationships to education to sex to spiritual life to many other topics and things in between, *Everything You Need to Know Before College* is still not *quite* complete. There's information and thoughts about the college life that I have yet to discuss and ramble on about. So that's why I've included *this* chapter.

Think of this chapter as that one lonely, undefined box you'll load into your mother's minivan when the moving-to-college time comes. Most of the boxes you'll have packed will be labeled with categories such as clothes, food, toiletries, books, CDs, school supplies, and so on written across the tops. But every college student always packs one box that gets "miscellaneous" written across the top.

You write miscellaneous on it because each item in the box, if it stood alone, would not fill an entire box. But the thought of leaving any of those items behind is incomprehensible. Consider this chapter to be just like *that* box.

You see, certain parts of the college experience are hard to put under a particular topic. So I decided early on that this would become the literary container for all information undefined or too defined to put in other chapters. You can already tell that this chapter is going to be fun, right? So here it is: Matthew Paul Turner presents "the miscellaneous chapter of a lot of lists." (Cue the drum roll, and push the applause button.)

EVERYTHING YOU'LL NEED TO PACK, BUY, AND BRING WITH YOU*

Grab your purse or wallet, your mom, a large vehicle, and a really big shopping cart. Wal-Mart, Target, IKEA, and other fine retailers are waiting for you to come spend your and your parents' money like mad. But before you go, you'll need a good list. But don't waste your time; I've written down a shopping list for you. You probably won't have to buy *all* of these items; you might already have some of them lying around the house. So look over this list, check your *personal* inventory, add the items that are not listed below, and get your butt shopping.

FOR YOUR DORM ROOM
[ ] Pictures/posters

[ ] Refrigerator (you might be able to rent this from school)

[ ] Storage cubes

[ ] Mirror

[ ] Dry erase board

[ ] Under-bed storage boxes

[ ] Closet organizers

[ ] Hanging organizer

---

* You might not need everything on these lists, so plan accordingly.

[ ] Fan

[ ] Clothes hangers

[ ] Bedspread

[ ] Two sets of bed sheets (be sure to have the proper size!)

[ ] Mattress cover

[ ] Two pillows

[ ] Small area rug

[ ] Small microwave (check with your roommate first)

[ ] Paper plates/bowls

[ ] Coffeemaker

FOR YOUR DESK

[ ] Dictionary

[ ] Thesaurus

[ ] Stapler/staples

[ ] Paper clips

[ ] Scissors

[ ] Notebooks

[ ] Ruler

[ ] 3x5 cards

[ ] Stackable desk trays

[ ] Pencils/pens

[ ] Highlighter pens

[ ] Pencil sharpener

[ ] Rubber bands

[ ] Address book

[ ] Stationery

[ ] Stamps

[ ] Calendar/daily planner (you might need more than just one)

[ ] Masking tape

[ ] Telephone

[ ] Answering machine

[ ] Calculator (if you're getting a Bachelor of Science, you might need a special kind of calculator)

FOR YOUR LAUNDRY

[ ] Laundry bag (takes up much less room than laundry baskets)

[ ] Detergent

[ ] Fabric softener

[ ] Dryer sheets

[ ] Stain remover

[ ] Lint remover

[ ] Bleach

[ ] Iron

[ ] Ironing board

[ ] Clothes brush

FOR YOUR CLEANING SUPPLIES

[ ] Dishwashing liquid

[ ] Dishcloth

[ ] Drying towel

[ ] Pre-treated cleaning cloths

[ ] Paper towels

FOR YOUR SEWING KIT

[ ] Thread

[ ] Needles

[ ] Pins

[ ] Small scissors

[ ] Safety pins

[ ] Container for sewing kit

FOR YOUR FIRST AID KIT

[ ] Bandages

[ ] Antiseptic

[ ] Pain killer/fever reducer

[ ] Cold/allergy medicine

[ ] Anti-gas medication

[ ] Anti-diarrhea medication

[ ] Prescription medication

[ ] Vitamins

[ ] Contact lenses

[ ] Contact lens supplies

[ ] Thermometer

[ ] Tweezers

FOR YOUR ELECTRONICS/TOOL NEEDS

[ ] Computer

[ ] Printer

[ ] Cables for computer and printer

[ ] Ethernet cables (unless your school uses Wi-Fi; you should find out)

[ ] Camera (and film if your camera is not digital)

[ ] Television (check with your roommate first)

[ ] DVD player

[ ] Video game equipment

[ ] CD player

[ ] iPod/MP3 player and equipment

[ ] Clock radio

[ ] Flashlight

[ ] Batteries

[ ] Hammer

[ ] Screwdriver

[ ] Pliers

[ ] Surge protector

[ ] Power strip (you might need more than one)

[ ] Stick-on wall hooks

[ ] Thumbtacks

[ ] Long cord for telephone

[ ] Desk lamp

[ ] Clip-on lamp for headboard

FOR YOUR BATHROOM NEEDS

[ ] Shower caddy (a small basket that will carry all of the following)

[ ] Soap

[ ] Shampoo

[ ] Conditioner

[ ] Toothbrush

[ ] Toothpaste

[ ] Tissue

[ ] Razor

[ ] Shaving cream

[ ] Deodorant

[ ] Flip-flops

[ ] Washcloths

[ ] Bath towels

[ ] Deodorizer

NiNE BRANDS EVERY COLLEGE STUDENT SHOULD KNOW

According to a number of recent studies, nearly 90 percent of return-ing college students can name a popular brand. Nike and Coca-Cola topped college students' lists for favorite brands. Brands no doubt connect with college students. The following nine brands might not be at the top of the list, but they are ones you should know.

1. APPLE. With laptops, iPods, podcasting, and Safari, Apple creates products and technology that enhance the college experience. Find out more at www.apple.com.

2. ART.COM. From serious art to silly pictures meant to make you laugh, www.art.com has it all for affordable prices.

3. CURRENT TV. Current is a TV news network for young adults who are concerned about the topics that FOX News and CNN cover but who don't relate to the perspectives. With a solid web base, interesting journalists, and a growing blogosphere, Current TV is a brand of television worth knowing about.

4. GT BICYCLES. As one of the leaders in the world of biking, GT Bicycles is changing the way students get around on campus. Check out gtbicycles.com for more information on the bikes as well as pricing and available styles.

5. IKEA. Whether you're decorating your dorm room walls, giving that shared bathroom a bit of pizzazz, or creating the perfect room for study-ing, www.ikea.com can help make an ordinary space come alive.

6. JAMBA JUICE. The all-natural-ingredient smoothie franchise has become a popular destination in many college towns. From information on its "shot of grass" or its freshly squeezed orange juice, find out more at jambajuice.com.

7. LOGOS. If you're going to college to study religion, Bible, or Old or New Testament history, the technology available at www.logos.com will be most helpful to you in your quest to understand theology.

8. NALGENE. Water has never looked better than when it's contained within a Nalgene bottle. Whether it's for sports, fun, or class, your drink will always be considered cooler in a Nalgene bottle. Find out more at www.nalgene-outdoor.com.

9. RELEVANTMAGAZINE.COM. Boasting one of the most popular Internet sites for Christian college students, RelevantMagazine.com combines spirituality and pop culture to create a compelling website about life in college.

THE MOM AND DAD SECTION (SHOW THIS TO THEM)
(Because parents need a little help, too)

Dear Parents,
This short section is for you.
Love, Matthew

PS: You're gonna do fine!
PPS: Oh yeah, your kid needs you to send money.

SIX THINGS YOU CAN DO TO MAKE YOUR COLLEGE STUDENT'S HEART SWELL IN LOVE AND APPRECIATION FOR YOU

1. SEND MAIL. Students' hearts skip a beat when they get mail. Usually, even junk mail makes them feel like somebody in the world loves them.

2. SEND CARE PACKAGES. Packages are to students what gazelles are to cheetahs. (Look on page 206 to see what the requirements are for a perfect care package.)

3. SEND MONEY. If you send money, your son or daughter will forget *all* about the fact that you have failed to send a care package.

4. SEND E-MAILS. But please don't send us those stupid forwards your silly old friends send you. We want *actual* e-mails from you. And you're allowed to e-mail only two pictures of your pets a month. *No more!*

5. SEND MONEY. Did I mention your kids are totally open to forgiving you for not showing up at their sixth-grade soccer game?

6. SEND LOVE. Most important, parents, love the heck out of your kids.

PUTTING TOGETHER THE PERFECT CARE PACKAGE

SIZE MATTERS. Don't wimp out on your kids! All care packages should be at least 10 inches by 14 inches by 8 inches. Anything less is no longer a care package and will not be counted as such.

CONTENT MATTERS. Fill it up with all the things that your kid loves. Think variety. Think candy, crackers, and other types of snack food. A check somewhere in there would be nice, too.

HOW IT'S DECORATED MATTERS. Write a bunch of fun messages on the outside of the box. Make all the other kids jealous about how much your kid is loved.

HOW YOU SEND IT MATTERS. Whatever you do, make sure it gets there within two days. No one wants stale cookies or a package that looks like it's gone to Asia and back. UPS and FedEx are good options.

HOW OFTEN YOU SEND ONE MATTERS. Remember, your kid gets very little mail. When he or she gets a package from you, it will literally make your child's day. He may never let you know how much it means to him, but trust me; he absolutely loves it.

SOME RANDOM ADVICE FROM COLLEGE STUDENTS ALL ACROSS THE COUNTRY
(Because hearing other people's advice really helps sometimes)

Treat college like work—get up and spend eight hours either in class or studying each day, even if it is just reading or studying notes from lectures. That way you'll have at least 40 hours in each week, and you shouldn't need to cram for tests. That'll give you evenings and weekends free for all that other stuff that you need time for in college. The best part is, if you get into this habit, you'll be so much more prepared for life after college, which can be a huge and devastating shock to the system.

—ERIC, 23

Sharing a dorm room with your best friend can be the worst thing in your life. There are a few that have stood the test of time and found it wonderful to room with each other, but for the most part it is a good idea to just get in the same building, not the same room, as your best friend! It does make a difference who your roommate is, so pick a friend who you know is fun but who will not borrow your clothes without asking! I was walking on campus one day and ran into my roomie, and she was wearing my new shirt that I had never worn. She hadn't asked me first whether she could wear it. I was so upset . . . we had a huge blowout, but it didn't seem to stop her unwelcome sharing. There are just some personalities you can live with and some you have to live apart from!

—DARCI, 24

Dump your high school girl/boyfriend.

—JEFF, 22

All I can say is, college is the best four/five years of your life. Really. High school was fun, true, but college is your last time to have those wild, carefree nights. Talk to the people sitting next to you in class. Befriend them. You already have that class in common, anyway. And when you go out, do as much as you feel comfortable doing. Important: DON'T BE PRESSURED INTO SOMETHING YOU'RE NOT COMFORTABLE WITH. KEEP YOUR MORALS, ETHICS, AND BELIEFS INTACT.

—ROBYN, 24

Meet as many different people as you can, and get involved with a good group of believers. Your life outside of college in a new city is even more important than school.

—ALLY, 27

Don't take advantage of your independence. Be able to let God write your story; after all, it's not about you. Be real with yourself and don't pretend to be something you're not.

—DAN, 21

If you don't like going to class, then don't go to college.

—PATRICK, 22

Sleeping in a big class is better than not going. The people sleeping next to you will become your support network.

—CHRIS, 25

Simple, I know, but have a separate notebook for each class.

—SCOTT, 22

Take good notes; most of my professors pulled their exam questions straight from their notes.

—ALYSON, 23

THREE COLLEGE STUDENTS SHARE THE GREATEST TRUTH THEY LEARNED IN COLLEGE

MY GREATEST TRUTH LEARNED: *That I was stronger and wiser than I gave myself credit for. That I wasn't as smart and strong as I gave myself credit for. And that I'll be relearning those lessons over and over my whole life. The assumptions we make about ourselves and then accept as set in concrete are some of the most dangerous we make in life, because they keep us from growing and discovering new aspects of our personalities.*

—SHARON, 47

MY GREATEST TRUTH LEARNED: *College is where I learned that any of us really have only two things to give: our love and our time. Give both freely, but not cheaply.*

—MIKE, 24

MY GREATEST TRUTH LEARNED: *You can probably find out a lot more about who God is once you leave Bible college than while you're in Bible college.*

—MICHAEL, 33

ONE AND A HALF VERSES FROM JOHN 8 THAT EVERY COLLEGE STUDENT SHOULD KNOW

"If you stick with this, living out what I tell you, you are my disciples for sure. Then you will experience for yourselves the truth, and the truth will free you." (verses 31-32)

SOME FINAL THOUGHTS ABOUT COLLEGE BEFORE YOU CLOSE THIS BOOK AND SET IT BESIDE YOUR TOILET
(Because a book about college needs a cheesy, inspirational ending— and it should be set beside the toilet)

When I graduated from college, I remember looking up into the bleachers where Mom and Dad sat. I felt completely overwhelmed with excitement. My mother's big smile lit up the auditorium. My father's confident smirk made me well up with pride. When my name came over the loudspeaker, the cheering began. As I got to the stairs to make my way off stage, I hesitated for a moment, just enough time to bring my tassel from one side of my hat over to the other. And as I walked across the stage at my commencement, the president of my college handed me a diploma. My friends and family in the crowd screamed with delight, and it was one of the most beautiful sounds I had ever heard. A large part of me couldn't believe I had finally arrived at a day that would mark my ability to forever look in the mirror and call myself a college graduate. It was indeed a powerful moment.

When I received that diploma, every experience I had encountered in college was present with me. A large part of the person I had become was the sum of all the events, people, and memories from my college career.

The relationships I encountered, whether they were close friends, professors I dearly valued, or people who were simply good acquaintances, affected the "me" who walked across that stage. Each person had helped mold and influence me in big and small ways. And all the things I did — both the good and the bad — walked with me on that day, too.

As you begin your college journey, remember that every part of this upcoming experience will become a part — maybe big or maybe small — of your college whole. Each part of this journey — every event, class, friendship, silly mistake, leadership role, personal best, calcu-lated mistake, and whatever else may come your way—will have a valu-able impact on the man or woman who you will eventually become.

Don't take these moments for granted. As you journey, make a point to hold on to your past, your values, and truth. But don't stop there. Take these upcoming experiences and use them, invest in them, learn from them, and grow with them. I believe it's these kinds of actions that lead a person to live the kind of life that will one day reap the benefits of choices made, lessons learned, and growth defined.

As you plant your seeds and seeds become planted inside you, resist the temptation to expect perfection. Be free enough in your faith and your personality to fail once in a while. Don't pursue failure, but don't fear it, either. You'll soon learn that many of your biggest mistakes will also teach you your greatest lessons.

Most of all, cling to God with all of your might, and let Him cling to you, too. No matter where life takes you, believe that His strong hand is able to reach that far and farther if needed.

This book is called *Everything You Need to Know Before College*, a gutsy title that I'm not sure is truly possible. Oh, I've come close to fill-ing this book with everything you'll need to know. It's certainly filled with a whole bunch of good information about going to college. And I hope it helps you in your adventure. But really, no one knows exactly what each individual will "need to know" during his or her college expe-rience. Sure, I can make some pretty good guesses. But a lot is still very uncertain. I believe it's the uncertainty that makes the college experi-ence so incredibly captivating and exciting. Not knowing the coming adventures, trials, and lessons will sometimes test our wisdom, faith, and truth. And that's good.

But through those trials and adventures you will face in college, do yourself a favor; spend a lot of time in prayer.

And then do some journaling.

But don't stop there. Get involved. Learn. Experience new things.

Grow. Trust. Fall down a few times. Make lots of friends. Scream at the top of your lungs once in a while. Be passionate. Build some bridges. Find someone to love. And be free enough to learn something new every day.*

The end (for me)

The beginning (for you)

---

* So, I leave you with another cheesy *Full House* moment. I began the book that way; I might as well close the book that way, too. In fact, "Danny Tanner" moments are pretty much dabbled throughout this book. But why do you care? Shouldn't you be packing or something?

NOTES

1. Kathleen Haughney and Leann Frola, "Study: 1 in 2 Sexually Active College Students Get STD," *The Arkansas Traveler*, April 12, 2004, http://www.thetraveleronline.com/media/paper688/ news/2004/04/12/News/Study.1.In.2.Sexually.Active.College .Students.Get.Std-657066.shtml?norewrite&sourcedomain=www. thetraveleronline.com.

2. Gary Gately, "College Students Ignoring Risks of Unprotected Sex," *Health on the Net Foundation*, August 22, 2003, http://www.hon.ch/ News/HSN/514693.html.

3. Dr. Bob Kizlik, "Effective Study Skills," September 19, 1997, http:// www.adprima.com/studyout.htm (last updated March 1, 2005).

4. Kizlik, "Effective Study Skills."

ABOUT THE AUTHOR

NAME: Matthew Paul Turner

AGE: 32

YEARS IN COLLEGE: 5

YEAR GRADUATED: 1996 (the years after college go by *really* fast)

COLLEGES ATTENDED: 2 years at Chesapeake College (Maryland); 3 years at Belmont University (Tennessee)

MAJOR: BBA with an emphasis in Music Business (I'm really using it, huh?)

BEST ADVICE GIVEN: "Get around people who are smarter than you and learn from them."

WORST ADVICE GIVEN: "You should try to find a wife in college."

I WISH I HAD KNOWN: That *trying to mix* the best and worst advice I was ever given would fail miserably.

A GREAT TRUTH: Just like everything in life, college is a journey of ups, downs, good times, and foolishness. It's who you choose to run to for peace, hope, and truth that is what really matters in the end.

OTHER BOOKS IN THE WORKS: *What You Didn't Learn from Your Parents About: Sex* and *What You Didn't Learn from Your Parents About: Christianity* (both TH1NK; watch for them in September 2006)